THE SKINHEAD INTERNATIONAL
A WORLDWIDE SURVEY OF
NEO-NAZI SKINHEADS

Anti-Defamation League
823 United Nations Plaza
New York, NY 10017

This publication was prepared by Irwin Suall, Director of Special Projects;
Thomas Halpern, Acting Director, Fact Finding Department; Mira Boland,
Washington, D.C. Fact Finding Director; David Rosenberg, Assistant Director,
Fact Finding Department; and James Q. Purcell, Assistant to the Civil Rights
Director.

**Copies of this report are in the Rita and Leo Greenland Human Relations
Library and Resource Center.**

All drawings contained in this report are taken from the publications, leaflets and record albums of neo-Nazi Skinheads
and extremist groups with which Skinheads are allied. They are included here to convey to readers the authentic flavor of
the printed material circulated among the Skinheads.

Cover photos:
Map of Europe in Gold Tones © Paul Ambrose 1994.
Skinhead © Reuters/Bettman

CONTENTS

FOREWORD

The unspeakable Oklahoma City bombing of April 19 brought home to the American people, like no other event in memory, the tragic lesson that no country is immune from terrorism. Although those charged with the bombing are widely thought to have had ties to larger extremist groups, the actual explosion appears to have been the work of a relative few. Here lies a second important lesson of Oklahoma City: it does not take a mass movement to perpetrate the most horrible kinds of crimes.

These thoughts seem relevant to the report which follows. Nowhere do the neo-Nazi Skinheads by themselves constitute a mass movement, although in many countries they do have links with broader political forces. But the paramount danger posed by these young racist thugs lies in their proven taste for violence. As the following pages show, neo-Nazi Skinheads across the globe have committed numerous murders, firebombings and other crimes of violence against innocent victims whom they deemed to be of the "wrong" race, religion, nationality or sexual orientation. Their goal, whether in Los Angeles, Berlin, Sydney, or São Paulo, is a "racially pure" society of the kind that prevailed in the Third Reich.

The Anti-Defamation League has paid close attention to the Skinhead movement ever since it first arose in the United States in the mid-eighties. Through a series of published reports we have tried to keep the American public informed of the activities of this movement. At meetings with successive U.S. Attorneys General, we have stressed that the Skinhead propensity for violent hate crimes warrants the close attention of the Department of Justice. Similar representations have been made to the appropriate law enforcement authorities on the State and local levels.

From the start, the Anti-Defamation League has been aware that the Skinheads are an international phenomenon. Hence this survey. It is designed to reveal to all concerned the global dimensions of this growing neo-Nazi menace. In light of the recent demonstration of the dangers posed by armed extremism, the report which follows seems more timely than ever.

David H. Strassler
ADL National Chairman

Abraham H. Foxman
ADL National Director

FINDINGS

Neo-Nazi Skinheads are bigotry's shock troops in much of today's world. They are street fighters for the xenophobia that has plagued so many nations. They thrive on violence, proclaiming hatred a virtue and criminal assaults as heroic. In Germany, they have mobilized against the Turks; in Hungary, Slovakia and the Czech Republic, the Gypsies; in Britain, the Asians; in France, the North Africans; in Brazil, the Northeasterners; in the United States, racial minorities and immigrants; and in all countries, homosexuals and those perennial "others," the Jews. In many places the targets include the homeless, drug addicts and others who are the down-and-out of society.

The neo-Nazi Skinhead movement is active in no fewer than 33 countries on six continents. It numbers some 70,000 youths worldwide, of whom half are hard-core activists and the rest supporters.

The countries where Skinheads are found in the greatest numbers are Germany (5,000), Hungary and the Czech Republic (more than 4,000 each), the United States (3,500), Poland (2,000), the United Kingdom and Brazil (1,500 each), Italy (1,000 to 1,500), and Sweden (over 1,000). France, Spain, Canada and the Netherlands each have at least 500 Skins. They are found in somewhat lesser numbers elsewhere in Europe and South America, and in South Africa, Japan, Australia and New Zealand.

The Skinhead movements in these various countries are extensively linked with each other. This "Skinhead International" is maintained through the travels abroad of popular Skinhead rock bands and their fans; the world-wide marketing of Skinhead paraphernalia and recordings; the sale and trading of publications known as "skinzines"; the wide exchange of propaganda materials and other correspondence; and, increasingly, the utilization of electronic communications — the Internet and computer bulletin board services.

In addition to links with their counterparts abroad, Skinheads in many countries have had domestic connections with neo-fascist political parties. Some such ties have been openly sought and acknowledged; others kept hidden from public view. Many right-wing parties value the youthful zealotry and muscle of the Skins, but are nervous about their unpredictable behavior. Thus, the connections vary considerably — some are overt, others covert, and they are subject to frequent change. The following are some of the far-right parties with which Skinheads have had links:

Belgium.................Vlaams Blok
Czech Republic.....Republican Party
France...................Parti Nationaliste Français et Européen (PNFE)
Germany...............Free German Workers Party (FAP, now banned);
                             German National Democratic Party (NPD)
Hungary................Hungarian Interest Party (MEP)
Italy......................Movimento Sociale Italiano (MSI)

Netherlands..........Centrumdemocraten (CD); Centrumpartij '86
          (CP '86)
Poland..................Polish National Community/Polish National Party
          (PWN/PSN)
Spain.....................Juntas Españolas
Sweden..................Sweden Democrats
United Kingdom...British National Party
United States.........Populist Party

Violence, Not Votes

Although willing to connect with these far-right parties, the Skinheads themselves reject the parliamentary road to power. Rather, they aim to achieve their goals by destabilizing society through the direct application of violence and intimidation. In those instances where the Skins have had a major impact, it is largely because their views were shared by a broader segment of the population. With their Molotov cocktails and cries of "Foreigners out," they have expressed in extreme form what a segment of the population in many countries has been feeling.

Nowhere has this been more the case than in Germany. The euphoria brought on by the collapse of the East German regime and the re-unification of the country soon gave way to strains that revealed large numbers of people deeply shaken by the uncertainties they faced. The world witnessed in some German towns shocking displays of support for Skinhead arson attacks on the residences of refugees and guest workers. While those who cheered Skin thuggery were far outnumbered by the masses of people who later engaged in vigils against the violence, the Skinheads could easily have perceived that they were acting out the inner wishes of many of their countrymen.

The German government's initial delay in effectively responding to the Skinhead threat no doubt contributed to the growth of the movement. Gains at the polls by far-right political parties, limited though they were, further emboldened the younger racists. The Skins had become the shock troops of a malevolent anti-foreigner groundswell, and it has taken considerable effort on the part of German law enforcement and concerned members of the public to begin to curb the menace.

Similarly, in the Czech Republic and Hungary, Skins have been viewed by some members of the community as their protectors because they attack Roma (Gypsies), a group that is popularly blamed for much of the crime. Roma and others regarded as aliens have found themselves surrounded by frenzied drunken Skinheads who maim them with crude weapons such as boots, bats, knives and iron rods. Certainly there is popular opposition to these attacks, but there is also some support, particularly if the attack follows an incident in which a Gypsy is blamed — rightly or wrongly — for a local crime.

U.S. Impact

By contrast, the danger posed by neo-Nazi Skinheads in the United States lies not in their public support, which is nil, but in their demonstrated willingness to kill and wreak havoc. They have been responsible for no fewer than 37 murders (of racial minorities, homosexuals, even other Skinheads), and wherever their gangs have surfaced, hate-motivated crime has invariably followed. Further, the Skinheads appeared on the American scene in the mid-eighties at a time when most racist and anti-Semitic groups, including the Ku Klux Klan and paramilitary neo-Nazi sects, were in decline. The new faces and raw energy of the Skinheads provided a shot in the arm for the organized hate movement in America.

In some countries, Skins have devised plans to spread terror through the use of sophisticated weapons rather than through riots and gang fights. In Sweden, for example, well-organized Skin gangs have constituted veritable terrorist organizations. They have raided arms depots, robbed banks and planted powerful explosives in an avowedly armed struggle to create their racist vision of Sweden's — and Europe's — future.

Ties to Other Thugs

The Skins often rely upon a ready reserve of other violence-prone youth as allies in their campaigns of intimidation and destruction. Chief among these are the football (soccer) hooligans, who have engaged in rioting in stadiums across Europe.* It is actually often difficult to distinguish between the Skins and hooligans, especially where the "hools" have taken on some of the characteristics of the Skins. Indeed, it often serves no purpose to distinguish between the two, as they operate similarly and at times in concert. Both Skins and hooligans can be found, for example, waving Nazi banners and chanting bigoted slogans at football matches.

A phenomenon similar to the relationship between Skinheads and soccer hooligans exists on the musical front. Through their music, some Skinhead rock bands have succeeded in attracting large non-Skinhead followings.

Apart from Skinheads and their near cousins among football hooligans and Skin music fans, there are young people in many of the countries in this survey that harbor similar bigoted attitudes and have demonstrated the capacity to act on them. Desecrations of Jewish cemeteries, for example, are as likely as not to have been committed by unaffiliated youths. But it must also be said that, judging by their handiwork, some of these freelance vandals take their cue from the Skins.

In sum, while it is nowhere a serious threat to the established order, the Skinhead movement has shown that it can inflict damage to the fabric of civil life. It engages in murderous assaults on innocent victims whose only crime is

---

*In a parallel to non-racist Skinheads, there have long been soccer hooligans who take part in brawls without necessarily espousing an extremist ideology or indeed any ideology at all.

that they are different. It is an extreme expression of the xenophobia that today plagues a large portion of the world. It exerts a baleful influence on the ideas and behavior of young people in many countries.

Through multiple links with their counterparts abroad, the use of modern electronic communications equipment, close alliances with football hooligans, connections with extreme right-wing political parties, and the promotion of racist music, the Skinheads have clearly shown that they warrant serious public concern.

THE SKINHEAD SCENE

The Skinhead phenomenon originated in England where gangs of menacing-looking, shaven-headed and tattooed youths in combat boots began to be seen in the streets in the early 1970's. Their style was meant to symbolize tough, patriotic, working-class attitudes in contrast to the supposedly sissyish, pacifist, middle-class views of the hippies.

The racist and chauvinist attitudes that prevailed at the time among many Skinheads later evolved into a crude form of Nazism. From the start, Skins drew public notice for their bigotry and taste for violence, exemplified by their frequent assaults on Asian immigrants, attacks which came to be known as "Paki-bashing."

In the years that followed, the Skinhead movement* spread from England to the Continent and beyond. Racist Skinheads are found today in almost every industrialized country whose majority population is of European stock. Those attracted to the movement are almost uniformly white youths between the ages of 13 and 25, with males outnumbering females. While Skins retain the mythology of the movement's working-class origins, in reality they come from a broad range of socio-economic backgrounds.

The intimidating look favored by male Skinheads is instantly recognizable: a shaved head or closely cropped hair; jeans; thin suspenders or braces; combat boots; a bomber jacket, sometimes emblazoned with Nazi insignia; and tattoos of Nazi symbols and slogans. For security reasons, Skinheads sometimes adopt a less conspicuous look, by, for example, letting their hair grow out.

Most Skinhead gangs range in size from fewer than 10 to several dozen members. To those devoted to the movement, being a Skinhead is a full-time way of life and not simply adherence to a fashion. Skinhead activities dominate the social life — and the domestic life — of gang members: they often live in communal crash-pads and stick to themselves when out in public. The girls usually have Skinhead boyfriends.

Neo-Nazi† ideology combined with the gang lifestyle provides Skinheads with a seductive sense of strength, group belonging and superiority over others. Invocation of Viking imagery offers the Skinhead a perception of himself as a racial warrior. The Skinheads glorify Hitler and aspire to create his vision

---

*Not all youths with shaved heads or closely cropped hair are neo-Nazis. There are many young people across the globe who call themselves Skinheads and eschew bigotry (some are actively anti-racist). They look the same as their racist counterparts — without the Nazi insignia — and follow many of the same fashions including a taste for "oi" music, beer and violence. Indeed, both types of Skinheads have been known to attack each other. The term "Skinhead" when used in this report refers to the neo-Nazi or racist variety, unless otherwise specified.

† The Skins' neo-Nazi views are very much a mixed bag. Some believe in orthodox Nazi ideology, parroting the rhetoric of Hitler and his propagandists. Others adhere to a mixture of racism, populism, ethnocentrism and ultranationalist chauvinism, along with a hodgepodge of Nazi-like attitudes. There is thus a range of views that can fit comfortably within what we are calling the neo-Nazi Skinhead movement.

of a world-wide, pan-Aryan Reich.* These strands — a sense of power, of belonging, of destiny — combine to create the appeal the Skinhead movement holds for disaffected youngsters.

Skinhead violence differs little from one country to the next. When on the prowl, they seek out members of hated groups and attack them. While their means of attack varies, Skinheads take special pride in using their boots as weapons. Vandalism is another Skinhead specialty: they scrawl racist graffiti and desecrate Jewish synagogues, cemeteries and memorials to the Holocaust.

While some Skinheads have been known to use drugs, virtually all drink. Heavy beer consumption often precedes incidents of Skinhead violence.

Music and Magazines

A major aspect of Skinhead life is their devotion to bands that play white power "oi" music, a hard-driving brand of rock and roll whose lyrics pound home a message of bigotry and violence.† No other means of communication — neither the spoken nor written word — compares with oi music's influence on their outlook and behavior. Music is the Skinheads movement's main propaganda weapon and its chief means of attracting young recruits into its ranks. Skins maintain universal ties through their music, distributing recordings internationally and organizing concert tours and music fests that feature both domestic and foreign bands.

Record labels devoted to white power music produce and market recordings, and informal networks of enthusiasts exchange bootleg cassette tapes. The artwork on the jackets of Skinhead recordings is characteristically devoted to racist and violent images.

Concerts range from performances in local hangouts to international festivals that attract Skinheads from neighboring countries. At these festivals, swastika-emblazoned banners decorate the bandstands while Skinheads, arms outstretched, shout slogans like "Sieg Heil" and "White Power." In whatever context the bands play, the event often degenerates into a free-for-all of slam-dancing and scattered fistfights.

Also central to the Skinhead scene are their magazines (commonly called skinzines or zines), usually crudely written newsletters that focus on

---

* There are occasional instances in which racial and nationalist allegiances may conflict, as in Poland where many Skinheads are virulently anti-German. In such cases, historic antagonisms are stronger than the appeal of Skinhead solidarity.

† Non-racist Skinhead bands also call their music "oi," a Cockney greeting which is equivalent to "hey!" Their music is in fact quite similar to that of the racist Skins, but without the bigoted lyrics.

Skinhead bands and their recordings. The zines promote Skinhead ideology and advertise services popular among Skins such as tattoo parlors, clothing stores that sell Skin fashions, and oi music distributors. In addition, they announce concerts and other events of interest to Skinheads everywhere. Zines are published sporadically, and it is not unusual for some to fold after a few issues and for new ones to crop up.

The zines serve as a vital link between Skinheads in different countries. The publications generally maintain friendly relations internationally, carrying usually favorable reviews of foreign bands and detailing — with some delight — the exploits of their counterparts abroad.

The most commonly used propaganda items among Skinheads around the world are printed and sold by an American neo-Nazi, Gary Lauck of Lincoln, Nebraska, who publishes in 12 languages. Lauck supplies huge quantities of cheap colorful stickers bearing swastikas and incendiary slogans like "Deport Race-Mixers" and "Polska Na Zawsze Ziemia Aryjska!" ("Poland Will Forever Be Aryan!"). He also publishes a neo-Nazi tabloid (in many languages) which he markets to Skinheads and non-Skinheads alike.

Law enforcement authorities in Germany and elsewhere have long linked Lauck's material to numerous criminal acts. German prosecutors succeeded in bringing about Lauck's arrest when they sent out a warrant to 15 other European countries where Lauck was thought to have supporters. He was arrested in Denmark on March 20, 1995. Pending Lauck's extradition to Germany, he has been charged with distributing illegal propaganda and Nazi symbols, incitement, encouraging racial hatred and belonging to a criminal group.

Other mentors of the Skinheads include Tom Metzger, leader of the California-based White Aryan Resistance, who circulates his inflammatory tabloid *WAR* among Skinheads around the world. In addition, pamphlets denying the reality of the Nazi murder of six million Jews are eagerly read by Skinheads. One Holocaust-denial tract, the "Leuchter Report," is distributed in large quantities by German-born Canadian Ernst Zündel. Copies have been supplied to readers in Germany through Bela Ewald Althans, a Munich-based neo-Nazi.

In whatever form it takes — zines, music, slogans, propaganda — the rhetoric of Skinheads and their supporters is designed to encourage violence. As this report shows, turning the rhetoric of violence into action is the hallmark of Skinhead activity wherever the young gangs have surfaced.

CONCLUSION

The neo-Nazi Skinheads have neither the capacity nor any real interest in capturing state power. There is no prospect that they will somehow, somewhere, create a "Skinhead Republic." What the Skinheads do have is a certain appeal for a limited number of young people in a great many countries. Much of the appeal, no doubt, lies in their cult-like qualities: their distinctive appearance, music, machismo, and the promise of fraternity they offer alienated youth. Yet the Skinheads are obviously no ordinary youth cult. Their Nazi ideology and violent behavior have caused fear and anguish in every community they have infested.

The Skins have been around long enough for Skinhead-watchers to make some informed judgments about how best to counter them. Above all, it is a serious mistake to remain passive during the early stages of their destructive behavior. A number of countries have learned this lesson the hard way — particularly Germany, whose initial half-hearted response to the Skinhead threat proved very costly. Its consequence was a dangerous escalation of Skinhead violence.

Having gone through that experience, Germany found that the most effective way to counter the Skinheads was through tough-minded law enforcement. Other nations learned the same lesson; in the United States, the Department of Justice formed a special Skinhead Task Force that succeeded in bringing about the trials and convictions of a number of American Skinheads. Both countries continue to face a serious Skinhead menace, but their tough law enforcement has resulted in a decline in the level of Skinhead violence.

The term "tough law enforcement" is not meant to imply the use of unlawful police methods. The laws defining hate crimes vary from one country to another, but their underlying principle is the same and it is sound: every democratic society has the right and duty to protect itself from the use of violence by those intending to destroy democracy.

Based on this survey, the Anti-Defamation League recommends:

1. Just as the Skinheads are linked across national borders, so should there be parallel police networking across borders wherever it does not yet exist. Such cooperation makes possible timely warnings of transnational plans for disruptive Skinhead activity at such events as soccer matches or oi music festivals. Similarly, within each country, law enforcement agencies should cooperate closely on Skinhead problems, particularly where there are separate jurisdictions on the federal, state, and local levels.

2. Racist music is the chief propaganda weapon of the Skinhead movement. In countries where the promotion of racism and Nazism is barred by law* the authorities ought to pay careful attention to the lyrics sung by

---

*Although constitutionally prohibited in the United States, such laws are commonplace in many, if not most, of the world's democracies.

8

Skinhead bands. Equally deserving of scrutiny are the record companies that produce and market this music. Their profiting from the sale of hate is especially despicable and warrants the rigorous enforcement of the anti-racism laws.

3. Our survey confirms that a pattern noted in the United States is occurring elsewhere: some Skinheads are shedding their standard look — letting their hair grow and changing clothes — in order to evade police surveillance. Good intelligence is needed when this occurs, because it may indicate that the Skins are going underground to hatch terrorist schemes.

The bottom line is that wherever Skinheads operate, their proclivity for hate and violence makes them a divisive and dangerous force in the community. The Anti-Defamation League urges citizens and governments alike to give these latter-day Nazi thugs the serious attention they deserve.

ARGENTINA

A racist Skinhead scene emerged in Argentina in the mid-1980's. Since then, its numbers have fluctuated and appear to have peaked in 1991 when they claimed approximately 100 Skinheads in Buenos Aires alone.

Many Argentine Skins harbor xenophobic views, blaming immigrants — some singling out Bolivians and Koreans — for the country's problems. Skinheads have also sparked violent confrontations in Buenos Aires clubs and discos, usually with other young toughs, particularly punk rockers. Nazi medals and tattoos are popular among Skins, and Nazi and racist graffiti attributed to them has appeared, occasionally written in English. Argentine Skins mix their cult of violence and hate with an enthusiasm for soccer and beer. As in Europe, it is often difficult to distinguish between Skinheads and soccer hooligans, and the two groups are known to overlap.

A neo-Nazi influence has pervaded the Argentine Skinhead movement from the start. Some Skins have been linked with Movimiento Nacional Socialista, a neo-Nazi organization.

Comando Suicida

The Argentine Skinhead movement has followed the fortunes of the Skin band Comando Suicida. Started in 1984, the band has folded and re-formed several times. Its lyrics (and interviews) express hostility toward immigrants, homosexuals, Catholics and Jews. The band has connections with Skinheads in Germany, and has been interviewed in English and Belgian zines. One of the band's members — formerly associated with Movimiento Nacional Socialista — offered the following commentary on contemporary Europe:

> Since World War II ended there's been a plot to destroy Europe, a racial destruction, I mean.... They filled Germany with Turks, France with Algerians, England with Pakistanis.... That's a way of filling Europe with shit, to mix, to mix them to spoil the good that is left in European blood.

AUSTRALIA

"Romper Stomper," an Australian motion picture that depicts savage violence by Skinhead toughs, has brought worldwide attention to Australia's Skinheads. Although the story on which the film is based is imaginary, there are indeed racist Skins Down Under and some of them actually liked the film. One such Skinhead has been quoted thus: "Up to a point it's against Skinheads ... but it's good publicity for our cause. With unemployment like it is, they're asking for trouble letting all these Asians into the country."

According to the Executive Council of Australian Jewry, Skinhead numbers have fluctuated over the past decade from a relative few to 300 to 400. There are Skinheads in most state capitols, some affiliated with such neo-Nazi groups as the Australian Nationalist Movement, Australian National Action, and the Australian National Socialist Movement. Both the Australian Nationalist Movement and Australian National Action succeeded in recruiting Skinheads in 1993 and 1994. As many as one-third to one-half of the participants in National Action rallies have been Skins.

White Australian Resistance

Two new racist Skinhead groups have made their appearance of late. One, a Sydney group calling itself Southern Cross Hammer Skinheads, has adopted the motto: "We must secure the existence of our people and a future for white children." (This expression, common among far-right activists in the United States, is known as "the 14 words," and was originally coined by David Lane, an American neo-Nazi terrorist serving a long prison term. It is noteworthy that the expression is now being used by an Australian Skinhead group which has also borrowed from its American cousins the term "Hammer Skinheads.") The other Skinhead gang, White Australian Resistance (WAR), located in Melbourne, apparently adapted its name from the California-based White Aryan Resistance (WAR). The head of the latter group, Tom Metzger, has boasted on his telephone hotline about the formation of the Australian organization.*

Aussie Skinheads have a record of violence similar to that of their counterparts the world over. From 1987 to 1989, National Action members in Sydney — some of them Skinheads — actively harassed anti-apartheid activists and members of homosexual organizations. On January 27, 1989, two National Action Skins fired bullets into the residence of the Sydney-based representative of the African National Congress.

In 1990, Special Branch detectives in Sydney concluded that Australian National Action had been encouraging Skinheads to mount "a campaign of terror" to distract attention from the Action group's own violent activities. The annual report of Australia's Security Intelligence Organization, released in May 1990, indicated that extreme right-wing groups had shown "a clear potential to cause distress to sections of the Australian community, and perhaps threaten life."

More recently, there have been further reports of sporadic Skinhead harassment of Asians and Jews. In Brisbane in May 1993, Skinheads of the Australian National Socialist Movement plastered the synagogue of the Brisbane Hebrew Congregation with posters and graffiti. In February 1994, four Skinhead females, chanting "Romper Stomper," attacked four Asian girls

---

*A Skinhead gang in Sweden has also adopted as its name the Swedish translation of White Aryan Resistance (Vitt Ariskt Motstånd).

with a knife and table-leg clubs at a Melbourne railway station. Train passengers were also reportedly harassed.

On March 26, 1994, some 20 neo-Nazi Skins in full regalia goose-stepped single file into a mall in downtown Adelaide shouting, "Sieg Heil" and "Heil Hitler." Their march soon turned into a rampage, resulting in at least 15 injuries and four Skinhead arrests. A passer-by said, "It was like a neo-Nazi riot in Europe you see on TV."

"Asian Invasion"

Several weeks later, Adelaide, still reeling from the Skinhead riot, was the scene of Australia's biggest neo-Nazi demonstration in several decades. The rally, sponsored by Australian National Action, included many Skinheads, along with bikers and other neo-Nazis. The 80 to 100 demonstrators gathered to denounce proposed anti-racist legislation. A nearby crowd of opponents hooted down National Action leader Michael Brander, as he railed against "the Asian invasion" and the "threat of Australia losing its identity to the Asian capitalists." Another National Action street demonstration, in an Adelaide suburb in December 1994, featured anti-Asian and other bigoted chants.

Australia's bloodiest Skinhead violence of the 1990's has pitted neo-Nazi Skins against each other (a common occurrence in other countries as well). In 1991, Skinhead Colin Irvine, whose bedroom was adorned with swastika flags and pictures of Hitler, allegedly murdered a fellow Skinhead, before being shot dead by police. On April 21, 1990, a National Action member in Sydney murdered a fellow Skinhead at a Hitler's birthday party. The victim, David Noble, of Adelaide, was killed by Skinhead Dave Sweetman, with the aid of fellow neo-Nazis Martin Bayston and Sean Shilling. During Sweetman's trial he shouted at journalists, "You Zionist maggots are going to get what you deserve. Sieg Heil!" Sweetman was convicted and is presently serving 20 years in Pentridge prison.

There is a limited Skinhead music scene in Australia. One band, Fortress, has produced a recording entitled "Seize The Day," according to the British skinzine *Last Chance*. Asked by *Last Chance* to describe the aims of Fortress, its spokesman replied, "The band follows a white racial/nationalist stance.... The songs are about being a Skinhead today, the plight of the white man ... heroes like Rudolf Hess." Other Australian bands mentioned from time to time in British and American zines have been Open Season and White Noise.

AUSTRIA

Since the mid-eighties Austria's Skinhead scene, while small and diffuse, has presented a threat to public order. In alliance with the "hools" (hooligans), gangs of Skins have terrorized soccer matches, disrupted youth centers and discos, and attacked random victims on the street and at subway stops. On most weekends the gangs gather at local pubs for drunken parties which frequently end in games of "hunt the foreigners."

Reporting on the knifing of two pedestrians on a Sunday evening in October 1990, a Viennese newspaper angrily noted that hardly a weekend passed without some act of criminal violence. In 1992, emboldened by events in Germany, the pace of such incidents quickened. A few examples will illustrate the trend:

In Graz, Skinheads went on a rampage following the arrest of some of their members by the police. Calling it "a revenge campaign," they left a trail of wrecked autos, smashed shop display cases and several distraught victims.

A band of neo-Nazis, including Skinheads, staged a provocative march through Innsbruck. A number of brawls broke out, ending with one of the neo-Nazis hospitalized with a skull fracture. Vowing revenge on the "leftist vermin," the gang invaded the hospital and threatened the staff. When police intervened, the gang left, shouting "Sieg Heil" and giving the Hitler salute.

In Salzburg, two Skinhead thugs assaulted two 15-year-old Yugoslav students

by shooting gas pistols in their faces. Both victims required hospitalization.

A gang of teenage Skinheads passing a synagogue on a Jewish holy day screamed at the congregation, "Long Live the Führer," "Down with the Jewish Swine," and "Death to the Jews." The Skins were later arrested and the ringleader sentenced to one year in prison.

The actual number of Skinheads in Austria is small in comparison with the surrounding countries. Perhaps 150 to 200 constitute the Skinhead scene and of these only a minority are activists. Because of their numerical weakness, they have formed a close relationship with the hooligans, resulting in a less politicized but more violence-prone movement. According to the skinzine *Stahlfront* (Steelfront), published in Steyr, the Skinheads number about 100 in Vienna, of whom only a hard core of 30 can be counted on. Their potential threat is enhanced by the 200 hooligans in the city with whom they often join forces. The same skinzine notes that in Linz, for example, the Skinhead presence is minimal, but the city is "terrorized by a large number of hools."

There are small, isolated bands of Skinheads in Wels, the Tirol and Steyr (a gang has recently re-emerged there led by the publisher of the zine *Stahlfront)*. The area around Graz (in particular the towns of Leoben and Zeltweg) is favored by Skinheads, much to the discomfort of the authorities. The Voralberg, next to Switzerland and southern Germany, is also a region with a noticeable presence of Skinheads. The town of Bregenz, near Lake Constance, for instance, was the site of a concert in 1992, featuring the German Skin band Störkraft and Dirlewanger from Sweden.

Austria has a native Skinhead music band, the Arbeiterfront (Labor Front), whose members are frequently in jail for a continuous string of violations. A second group, called Oisterreicher (word play on "Austrian" using "oi," the term for Skinhead music), has disbanded.

Skinhead Awake

A half dozen skinzines have circulated of late in Austria. One zine, *White Pride*, from Vienna, has been printed in English. The oldest and most

politically influential zine appears to be *Skinhead Erwache* (Skinhead Awake — Vienna). Others titles have been *Aufstand* (Revolt — Wels), *Pride of Austria, Heimatland* (Homeland — Pottendorf), and the aforementioned *Stahlfront* (Steyr).

In addition to relying on hools to inflate their numbers, the Austrian Skinheads depend largely on their German and other foreign counterparts for activities and inspiration. On May 11, 1992, about 80 Skins, many coming from Germany and Luxembourg, gathered at St. Pölten. A concert planned in Wels for August 31, 1992, at which Skinhead bands from Hungary, Germany and England were to appear, was canceled because the hall became unavailable, Instead, Austrian Skins traveled to Remblinghausen in Germany for a giant open-air concert with seven German Skin bands. Austrian Skinheads joined their German comrades at demonstrations in Gottingen on May 17, 1992, in Bielefeld (where they met at the National Front Center) and in Roth, where drunken Skins marched through the streets shouting "Foreigners Out!"

Austrian Skinheads are also closely allied with Hungarian Skins. Groups frequently travel to Budapest to dance at the popular Viking Club, join the Hungarian hools at soccer matches, or meet with their comrades for beer parties. The Hungarian Skin bands Egészséges Fejbőr (Healthy Skinhead) and Pannon Bulldog are highly popular and T-shirts bearing their logos are avidly worn by Austrian Skins.

Austria's Skinheads are favored by hardly any political groups except Gottfried Küssel's National Extra-Parliamentary Opposition Party (VAPO). Küssel, now in prison for his neo-Nazi activities, has aggressively canvassed support among the Skinheads and his literature is widely circulated in Skinhead ranks. The zine *Skinhead Erwache* carried on the front cover of issue No. 8 an old Nazi drawing of marching stormtroops with the rune-eagle of Küssel's VAPO replacing the swastika. Despite his ideological appeal, however, few Skins have actually applied for VAPO membership. On the other hand, most of Küssel's followers began their right-wing activity as Skinheads.

While small, the Austrian Skinhead movement ought not be ignored. It forms part of the larger neo-Nazi network that has developed between Austria and Germany and that believes in a future where Austria is once again united with a resurgent Reich.

BELGIUM

A small neo-Nazi Skinhead scene exists in Belgium, centered around Antwerp, the city with the largest following of the far-right political party Vlaams Blok (VB), or Flemish Bloc.

Neo-Nazi Skinheads in Antwerp congregate in cafes in the area of the Vrijdagmarkt, a well-known square. Their favorite haunt is reportedly a cafe called Gilby's, where Skins from Belgium, Holland, Germany and elsewhere mix with members of far-right Belgian groups including the Vlaams Blok, the Nationalistisch Studenten Verbond (Nationalist Student Association), Voorpost (Outpost) and Were Di (Protect Yourself). After a Hitler's birthday celebration at Gilby's in April 1993, some 20 Skinheads went to another cafe where they wrecked the interior and beat up two patrons.

Skinheads were at the center of an episode of rioting in the town of Sint-Niklaas in September 1993, in which an immigrant and a police officer suffered injuries. The incident occurred after a concert by a group called the Mushrooms. The police apprehended 41 Skinheads whom they later released and escorted out of town; none were from Sint-Niklaas, according to the police.

Vlaams Blok

In the political arena, Skinheads in Belgium are naturally drawn to the Vlaams Blok, the country's most significant far-right party. The VB, whose program is Flemish nationalist and anti-immigrant, won more than 10 percent of the Flemish vote — including over 25 percent in Antwerp — in the November 1991 parliamentary elections. The party received 28 percent of the Antwerp vote in the 1994 local elections, making it the largest party in the city.

Other far-right organizations with links to the Belgian Skinheads have included the Jonge Wacht (Young Guard), based in Antwerp and Ghent, and the francophone group L'Assaut (Attack), which dissolved in September 1993. Its leader, Hervé Van Laethem, attended a March 1993 gathering in Paris of more than 120 neo-Nazi Skinheads from across Europe. L'Assaut produced an eponymous monthly publication; following dissolution of the group, Van Laethem and others from L'Assaut began publishing a neo-Nazi sheet called *Devenir*, named for the French SS organ during World War II. Van Laethem died in 1994.

The British Skinhead organization Blood and Honour, which produces concerts and publishes a skinzine of the same name, has a Belgian Division. At least two Belgian skinzines have appeared: *Blind Justice*, in Liège, and *Pure Impact*, in Brussels. *Pure Impact* has also offered tapes of Skinhead music for sale.

The British skinzine *Last Chance* reported in early 1994 that two British bands, Squadron and Celtic Warriors, had a recent gig in Belgium abruptly halted halfway through the first band's set, possibly due to outbreaks of fighting. In August 1992, local authorities canceled a performance by the British Skinhead band Skrewdriver that had been scheduled for a Flemish nationalist event.

A number of Belgian Skinheads reportedly follow "Odinism," the worship of the Norse god Odin, a doctrine said to have a sizable number of adherents in the Vlaams Blok as well.

Ax Attack

Two Belgian Skinheads, Steve Frank Anthony Cirock and Clivo Bruno, and a Florida Ku Klux Klansman were involved in an October 1992 attack on a black man in northern Florida. The Belgians, who had come to the United States to attend a KKK gathering in North Carolina, joined their Florida host, Klansman Jack Bullock, in chasing the car of Benjamin Ross, whom they accused of stealing a pack of cigarettes from a convenience store. After ramming Ross's car with his pick-up truck, Bullock began shooting at him. The chase and the shooting continued on foot, while Cirock attacked Ross's car with an ax. Bullock was convicted of aggravated assault with a firearm and was sentenced to three and a half years in prison. Cirock, who returned with Bruno to Belgium, was charged with criminal mischief, a misdemeanor, which authorities deemed insufficient to warrant his extradition.

BRAZIL

A major theme of Brazilian Skins is hatred of *Nordestinos* (Northeasterners), people from the impoverished Northeastern states who have migrated in increasing numbers to the large cities in search of a better life. The issue parallels immigration problems in Europe and the United States, stimulating the same popular fears of job loss and insecurity. Brazil's racist Skinheads, like their counterparts elsewhere, thrive on such fears.

The largest concentration of Brazilian neo-Nazi Skinheads is in São Paulo, an industrial city of more than 10 million people. An estimated 1,000 Skins roam the city's streets behaving in the usual menacing Skinhead manner. Three separate groups operate in the city:

1. Carecas do Suburbio (Skinheads of the suburbs), a gang noted for its ultra-nationalism and gay-bashing, which hangs around bars in the eastern part of the city.

2. Carecas do ABC (ABC Skinheads), named for the initials of three industrial suburbs. They subscribe to the fascist doctrines of Plinio Salgado, the 1930's leader of the "Integralists." The ABC Skins are extremely violent and hostile toward Jews, homosexuals and Northeasterners.

3. White Power Skinheads, an avowedly Nazi gang that is the most violent of all. They hate Jews, blacks, homosexuals and Northeasterners, and advocate the secession of the more prosperous southern Brazil from the rest of the country.

Skinhead

São Paulo

100% violência

Elsewhere in Brazil, there are fewer Skinheads than in São Paulo, but they still present serious problems. In Rio de Janeiro, a neo-Nazi gang named Carecas do Brasil (Skinheads of Brazil) operates in the Bangu neighborhood. Other gangs are active in the city of Pelotas, in the southern state of Rio Grande do Sul; in Curitiba, the capital of the state of Parana; and in the cities of Florianópolis and Blumenau in the state of Santa Catarina.

Violent Lifestyle

Crimes of violence are intrinsic to the lifestyle of Brazil's Skinheads. Most such crimes are not reported, for the same reasons that crime generally is under-reported in Brazil. The criminal episodes listed below are but a portion of the whole.

In September 1992, two Jewish students from Beith Chabad were set upon and brutally beaten by 12 Skinheads. The assault took place in Santo Andre, a suburb of São Paulo.

During the same month, São Paulo Skinheads, shouting "Death to the Northeasterners," painted a red swastika on the wall of a cultural center for Northeastern migrants.

In November 1992, a black man sleeping on a bench in downtown São Paulo was seized and severely beaten by Skinheads shouting racist epithets.

São Paulo's Radio Actual has had racist slogans painted on its walls.

The station specializes in programs for Northeastern migrants.

Two Jewish cemeteries were desecrated in Porto Alegre, and the walls of the Jewish Society of Pelotas were covered with anti-Semitic slogans. Skinheads are believed to have been responsible.

In January 1993, 50 Skinheads scrambled aboard a São Paulo bus and assaulted its passengers. The week before, 40 Skinheads were arrested following a riot in Epinotec, a discotheque in downtown São Paulo.

In March 1994, members of the Carecas do ABC Skinhead gang murdered a 15-year-old black youngster, one of São Paulo's "street urchins."

The Brazilian federal government and the state of São Paulo have officially condemned Skinhead offenses, and, in many cases, have taken effective action against the gangs. In April 1994, the federal police began operating a new department specializing in crimes motivated by racism.

The Music Scene

Brazil's Skinheads listen to the same songs, performed by the same bands, as do Skinheads everywhere. Their fanzines, which list their favorite bands, offer a roster of names familiar to Skinheads around the world: the English bands No Remorse and Skrewdriver, France's Légion 88, Sweden's Ultima Thule, and others.

Two local Skinhead bands have arisen in Brazil. The better-known one, Locomotiva, is a São Paulo group. In a 1992 interview with a local fanzine, the band's spokesman, "Ivan," said the group had been influenced by the music of Skrewdriver, Brutal Attack and Peggior Amico (an Italian group). He said the band had one record on the market, "São Paulo Patria," produced by the French record company Rebelles Européens.

The other Brazilian band, GSB, was founded in 1990. Its initials stand for Grupo Separatista Branco (White Separatist Group). Less popular than Locomotiva, its views are openly Nazi.

Skinhead recordings are not readily available in music shops in Brazil, but can be obtained by mail order. One such mail order outfit operates out of a post office box in Santo Andre.

Two openly racist skinzines, *Orgulho Paulista* and *Determinacao E Coragem,* have made appearances in Brazil, with offerings of interviews, ratings of bands, and announcements about the Skinhead music scene. Both express admiration for such hate groups from the United States as the Ku Klux Klan, the Church of the Creator and Gary Lauck's neo-Nazi NSDAP-AO.

BULGARIA

A small Skinhead scene has been observed in Bulgaria in Varna, Pleven and the capital city of Sofia. Foreigners and Gypsies are the most frequent victims of Skinhead assaults. On March 26, 1994, a large gang of Skinheads attacked members of the Gypsy community in Pleven. The Skins reportedly beat several people and set one house on fire.

The 1994 Human Rights Report of the U.S. Department of State reports that Skinheads in Ruse attacked parishioners attending services at the Bulgarian Church of God. Eight people were seriously injured.

The youth wing of a group calling itself the Bulgarian National Socialist Party claimed responsibility for the distribution of pro-Hitler leaflets at a university in the summer of 1993, but it is not clear whether the organization has any connection to the Skinheads.

CANADA

An estimated 600 young people are involved in the neo-Nazi Skinhead movement in Canada. These include a hard core of some 350, plus an additional 250 who are, to varying degrees, participants or supporters. While their numbers were declining in the late eighties, that trend was reversed in the 1990's. The cities with the largest contingents of Skinheads are Toronto, Montreal, Ottawa and Vancouver, but activity has also occurred in recent years in Edmonton; Calgary; Winnipeg; Saskatoon; Regina; Quebec City; Halifax; Victoria, B.C.; Moncton, New Brunswick; and the Ontario cities of Kitchener, Windsor, Kingston and London.

Skinheads have been a part of Canada's extremist scene since the early 1980's. As in the United States, they have no national organization, operating instead in separate gangs with names like Aryan Resistance Movement Skins, Northern Hammerskins, and Final Solution Skinheads. Canadian Skins have also figured prominently in some established racist and anti-Semitic hate groups, such as the Heritage Front, led by Wolfgang Droege of Toronto; the Nationalist Party of Canada, headed by Don Andrews; the Church of the Creator, which originated in the United States; and the Aryan Nations, headquartered in Idaho.

Older white suprema-cists in Canada have regarded the Skinheads as potential recruits to bolster their flagging numbers. Performances by Skinhead bands have drawn young fans to rural rallies at which they have been lectured by such longtime extremists as John Ross Taylor (who died in November 1994) and one-time Canadian Nazi Party leader John Beattie.

Some of the rally sites have been provided by right-wing extremists, as in 1990 when 200 white supremacists, most of them Skinheads, gath-ered at Ian MacDonald's farm in Metcalfe, Ontario. There they were treated to the music of the British Skinhead band No Remorse, while armed Skins

Greig Reekie/Canada Wide

in military fatigues stood by. In other instances, land has been rented without signaling its intended use, as at Des Laurentides, Quebec, in 1992. The event, "Aryanfest '92," was sponsored by a Canadian unit of the Ku Klux Klan and attracted 70 Skinheads, including members of the Montreal neo-Nazi group, White Power Canada.

Aryan Nations

The leader of the Canadian branch of the Aryan Nations, Terry Long, organized a 1990 event billed as the "First Annual Alberta Aryan Fest," near Provost, Alberta. Neo-Nazi Skinheads, some of them armed, scuffled with Jewish protestors and assaulted a reporter.

Canadian Skinheads have been particularly active in the Heritage Front. The Front was formed in 1989 following a visit to Libya by 18 members of the extreme-right Nationalist Party of Canada. (The Nationalist Party members, jointly with 25 mostly left-wing Canadian activists, participated in a con-ference hosted by Libyan strongman Muammar Qaddafi.) Some of the 18 subsequently broke away to form a new organization. About six of the original 18 were Skinheads, including Peter Mitrevski, Jim Dawson and Max French, who have since assumed elevated roles in the Heritage Front. The leader of the Front, Wolfgang Droege, is a former Ku Klux Klansman who has served time in U.S. and Canadian jails for drug and weapons violations and assault. Over the course of the group's six-year existence, it has sponsored numerous rallies and demonstrations.

California Connection

White Aryan Resistance (WAR), led by Tom Metzger of Fallbrook, California, has exerted influence over Canadian Skinheads through direct contact, propaganda and speeches. Metzger and his son, John, traveled to Toronto in June 1992 to address a Heritage Front rally of some 200 people, many Skinheads among them. In February of that year, Metzger's associate, Dennis Mahon of Oklahoma, appeared at a Heritage Front rally attended by a similar number of Skins. Both the Metzgers and Mahon were deported from Canada. The name of an Ontario gang, the WARskins, suggests it has drawn inspiration, if not direction, from Metzger.

WAR's newspaper has promoted the activities of Vancouver Skinhead Tony McAleer, who has run a telephone message hotline in connection with an operation he calls Canadian Liberty Net. In April 1994, a Los Angeles radio station tried to send McAleer and John Metzger — anti-Semites both — to Germany for a broadcast on the Holocaust. German officials refused them entry. McAleer's Vancouver-area confederates include the Aryan Resistance Movement Skins and the Skinhead rock band Odin's Law. The two groups share a Surrey, B.C., post office box.

Racial Holy War

George Burdi, the leader of the Skinhead rock band Rahowa (shorthand for Racial Holy War), has recently created a record company, Resistance Records, devoted exclusively to the recording and distribution of "White Power" Skinhead rock music. Although Burdi is from Toronto, his company utilizes a Detroit, Michigan, post office box in order to avoid Canada's law against racist material.

Also known as "Reverend" Eric Hawthorne, Burdi, 24, has been a top figure in the Church of the Creator. The "church," whose late founder, Ben Klassen, dressed a package of racist, anti-Jewish and anti-Christian hatred in religious garb, has had several hundred members in the United States, Canada, Sweden and South Africa. Evidence suggests many of these Skins remain active white supremacists despite the recent disintegration of the American parent organization. Burdi now heads the youth wing of the Heritage Front.

Resistance Records has released a professionally produced CD and cassette by Rahowa, featuring such songs as "Third Reich," "Triumph of the Will," "Race Riot," and "White Revolution." Burdi boasts of having signed a number of other Skinhead bands, including Aryan, from London, Ontario, and the U.S.-based bands Aggravated Assault, Nordic Thunder, Bound For Glory, and Max Resist & the Hooligans. The label is aggressively marketing its product through a telephone hotline and a professional-looking publication, *Resistance*.

Other publications produced in recent years by Canadian Skins include *Canada Awake*, from Ottawa, and *The White Warrior*, from Montreal.

"Cowardly Attack"

Canadian Skinhead music has inspired countless acts of savagery by angry (and often drunken) Skinheads against minority group members. On June 6, 1993, shortly after attending a Rahowa concert at a Toronto area bar, Skinhead Jason Hoolans and some comrades went looking for a victim. They found Sivarajah Vinasithamby, 45, an immigrant who had taught math in his native Sri Lanka but was working as a dishwasher in Canada to support his family. Hoolans assaulted and repeatedly kicked his victim in the head in what the sentencing judge called a "totally unprovoked, vicious, cowardly attack" that left the victim brain damaged and partially paralyzed. Testifying in court, Hoolans described how he 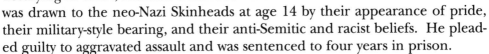 was drawn to the neo-Nazi Skinheads at age 14 by their appearance of pride, their military-style bearing, and their anti-Semitic and racist beliefs. He pleaded guilty to aggravated assault and was sentenced to four years in prison.

Canadian Skinheads have committed scores of other crimes as well, a sampling of which follows:

While jogging in a Montreal park in November 1992, Yves Lalonde, 51, was beaten to death by a group of Skinheads who thought he was a homosexual. Four Skinheads between the ages of 15 and 17 pleaded guilty to second-degree murder and received three years of detention, the maximum sentence for offenders under age 18. (Three of the Skins received two additional years of probation; the fourth, one year.) The killers' names were withheld because of their ages, in accordance with Canadian law. One of them was described in court as the "vice president" of a Montreal racist Skinhead gang.

Timothy Russell Biscope, 19, a Skinhead from Calgary, received a 19-year sentence for his part in the killing of a fellow Skinhead in northern Idaho in December 1992. Two Skins shot Johnny Ray Sharbnow, 29, a Michigan native, and enlisted the help of a third to dump his body in a remote location. The third accomplice, who led authorities to the site of the killing, said Sharbnow was shot in an argument that resulted when the car the four were driving to the Aryan Nations compound in Hayden Lake, Idaho, got stuck in the snow.

Keith Rutherford, a retired radio broadcaster, was confronted at his suburban Edmonton home in April 1990 by two Skinheads angry over a 30-year-old broadcast in which he had exposed an alleged Nazi war criminal. Rutherford was kicked in the groin and struck in the face with a club, causing serious damage to his eye. Charged in the attack were Daniel Sims and Mark Swanson, both 19 at the time. Sims, who appeared in court in an Aryan Nations T-shirt, received a 60-day sentence after pleading guilty to assault; Swanson got eight months for aggravated assault. The Crown Attorney later appealed Sims' sentence, and it was augmented to 18 months.

A Toronto Skinhead, currently serving prison time in the United States for a killing, is a suspect in a February 1991 robbery and assault on a fellow Toronto Skinhead that left the victim crippled. Jeffrey Paul Juczel allegedly beat and choked his victim, robbed him of cash and credit cards, and dragged him naked through the streets while continuing to beat him.

Daryl Sutton, a Toronto area racist Skinhead, was sentenced to prison in 1994 for the murder of David Murray Quesnel, 18, in a Toronto rooming-house after a night of drinking.

Concert Turns Violent

In May 1993, a planned concert by Rahowa in Ottawa brought out several hundred protestors. Following dispersal of the demonstrators, running battles broke out on Parliament Hill, resulting in assault convictions against a number of Skinheads, including Rahowa bandleader George Burdi, who was sentenced to one year in jail.

Canadian courts have held Skinheads responsible for a synagogue defacement in Toronto and the desecration of a Jewish cemetery in Hamilton, Ontario. Skinheads have also been linked to attacks on synagogues, cemeteries and other Jewish institutions in Montreal, Vancouver, Ottawa, Winnipeg, Quebec City, Calgary and Moncton.

CHILE

In Chile the Skinhead and neo-Nazi worlds blur and intersect, due to the existence of: (a) a sizable Hitlerite youth movement which is not necessarily marked by musical proclivities or shaved heads, and (b) *Cabezas Rapadas* — Skinheads — some of whom are neo-Nazis, and others ultra-nationalists given to street violence.

There are, however, obvious general tendencies which have led to interaction among the groupings. In the British skinzine *Last Chance*, Chilean Skinhead Hans Kwasigroch has written that many Skins are "non-political," although the rise of a deeply ideological neo-Nazi youth movement, "Esoterica," has led to "an awakening" in which most Skins can identify with the Nazis "in the same cause, the love of our country."

One of the leaders of the Nazis, a writer and former diplomat named Miguel Serrano, speaks ambiguously on the question of violence. "For now, we cannot take to the streets and fight," he says. "This is the time to defend our ideals, myths, and legends." As for the Skinheads: "I would tell them not to employ violence, simply because it is unnecessary. But if we keep bringing in Koreans, Taiwanese and Jews, violence will probably result." But Serrano has defended Skinhead assaults against homosexuals and drug addicts as "stupendous!" and has chided the Catholic Church for not doing more about such persons. "The Skinheads," says Serrano, "represent the most profound and important values of the Chilean people."

Core of Two Hundred

Over the past two years the Skins' numbers have grown in Chile's two major metropolitan areas, Santiago (particularly in its suburbs of Maipu and Puente Alto) and Valparaiso. The movement is estimated to comprise a core of 200 militants throughout the country.

Chile's Skinheads are said to be quite certain that a totalitarian system will one day be imposed upon the whole world, and that all people will see that it is best for them. The idea is articulated in their songs, which carry much the same fulsome thoughts as Skin music everywhere.

The most successful of the Chilean Skin bands, Rockan Oi, features a song dedicated to Hitler ("Someone Like You Will Never Be Forgotten"), which proclaims, in part: "He created a nation ... he only wanted to rid his country of worms."

Among Rockan Oi's other titles are: "KKK," "Camarada Rudolph Hess," and "One in a Million" (a reference to Nazi leader Serrano). Rockan Oi has played in theaters and at university campuses. As elsewhere, it is through their music at such gatherings that the Skins reach impressionable youngsters. The Santiago newspaper Mercurio has noted a serious influence of Skinhead "culture" on campus life, naming several universities: Chile, Central, Diego Portales, and Gabriela Mistral.

"Kick a Few People"

There is, of course, a rowdy side to the story. The Skinhead quoted from the British skinzine earlier wrote: "We go out to have a laugh and perhaps kick a few people who are not nice to us. We go to pubs or heavy metal concerts and every Friday and Saturday we end up really drunk."

Chilean Professor Erwin Robertson, an historian who is an unabashed admirer of Hitler, has found the Skinheads "an interesting phenomenon because they are middle-class youths, spontaneously organized, who have taken an attitude of rebellion."

COLOMBIA

The voices of members of the Colombian Skinhead gang GRAE ("Anti-Foreigners Skinhead Group") in Bogota, as quoted in the weekly journal *Semana* (June 1, 1993):

> "We are a group of young people of the extreme right. We are called Colombian National Socialists. And we are violent. We fight the drug addicts, vagrants, prostitutes."
>
> "We are not racists, but we believe that each [race] ought to stay in its place."
>
> "We are not copies of the German Skinheads. We don't have to read Hitler to love our country. We simply apply his ideas to our society."

The appearance of neo-Nazi Skinheads *(Cabezas Rapadas)* in Colombia is recent compared to other countries; the phenomenon drew notice no earlier than February 1993, when GRAE was formed in Bogota. The gang consisted of only seven members then, but their numbers had grown to 40 within a few months, and groups had sprung up in the provincial capital cities of Medellín, Pereira, and Cali. By late spring, their memberships totalled perhaps 80, the members' ages ranging from 16 to 25 years. Since then, however, the Skinhead scene has declined somewhat.

Skinhead Patrol

One rainy summer night the editors of *Semana* dispatched reporters to observe an evening's activities of members of GRAE in Bogota. The Skins set out to "patrol" the city at 10 p.m. "dressed in green trench coats, tight jeans, steel-toed army boots, and with their heads shaved...." Their aim: to make their presence felt at the favorite gathering places of the city's youth. During the next two or three hours, the reporters witnessed the gang's involvement in the following activities: smashing the windows of a tavern where some people were said to be using drugs; kicking a passerby whose T-shirt bore a U.S. flag ("He is a shitty Yanqui," they said); and finally beating and kicking four male transvestites until all four were unconscious. The reporters heard some cries of encouragement from people on the street: "Viva Colombia!" and "Onward with the cause!"

Foreigners are among the chief victims of the "cause." The Bogota Skins have assaulted natives of Ecuador and European visitors they brand as "hippies." The GRAE Skinheads say, "Colombia must be for the Colombians, and the pride of being born in this country must be restored." Other targets are the impoverished and the homeless. A member of GRAE gives his rationale for violence:

> What do we need indigents for? — or drug addicts or prostitutes? These people produce nothing. They only damage the image of our country. That's why we have to attack them — and the more we hit them, the better!

"Good Manners"

For all the dubious ethics of Skinhead tactics, GRAE is cautious about the "character" of prospective members and has rejected many. An acceptable member will either have a steady job or be a student, and will endeavor to be "the best at whatever he does." He will come from a healthy family, and will be neither an alcoholic nor an addict. "We want well educated people with good manners," says a member of the GRAE Skins.

There are other sorts of Skinhead gangs. One of the oldest and most violent originally concentrated its efforts on attacking prostitutes and indigents, but more recently named itself the "Anti-Animal Exploitation Skinheads" (REA) and planned to limit its future activity to ecological themes — possibly attacking laboratories where animal experiments are conducted, and attempting to put an end to bullfighting. The REA claims 45 members. Another of the smaller groups (without ecological concerns) reportedly has armed its members with pistols and other weapons. As for the Skinhead music, the popular British skinzine *Last Chance* has publicized two Colombian bands, Assault Detachment and Cerveza Amarza (Bitter Beer).

CZECH REPUBLIC

In the Czech Republic, as in other Central and Eastern European countries, the Gypsies (also known as Roma) — targets of Nazi extermination programs during World War II — have been facing a rising tide of racist hate. Skinheads, if not the most numerous among the racists, are often the most visible.

The primitive Skinhead racism in the Czech Republic is of the neo-Nazi variety. Although Czech Skins spew anti-Semitic rhetoric, the Roma are their chief targets. Others have been "guest workers" (mainly from Vietnam), Arab and African students, and foreign tourists. The Czech word *vycisteni* (cleansing) has come into wide use by the Skins and other hatemongers.

Estimates vary as to the number of Skinheads in the Czech Republic. Some observers estimate that between 800 and 2,000 are active in Prague, with several thousand more active in other cities and towns. Czech Police calculate that there are at least 400 in Prague and 3,000 to 4,000 nationally. The largest concentrations are in the industrial areas of northern Bohemia.

"Join!"

Skinhead Violence

April and May 1990, Prague and other cities. There were reports in April and May 1990 of Skinheads attacking groups of Gypsies with clubs and chains in several northern Bohemian cities. On May 1, some 200 Skins attacked Gypsies and foreign workers (mainly Vietnamese) in Prague's main square and afterwards assaulted a group of Canadian tourists.

February 1991, Prague. In a highly publicized case, a Czech sculptor, Pavel Oporensky, came upon a gang of Skinheads (including some Austrian Skins) that had just assaulted a passerby who had taunted them and viciously attacked another man who had come to his rescue. Jumping in to help, Oporensky was quickly surrounded by threatening Skins. While defending himself, he fatally slashed one of the gang with his pocket knife. He was tried for manslaughter, found guilty and sentenced to four years probation. Oporensky had been a Charter 77 dissident under the Communists and later lived in New York for 10 years. The victim, 17-year-old Ales Martinu, was buried in his Skinhead clothes while Orlik, a Skinhead band, performed.

October 1991, Teplice. Two Gypsies in an automobile were attacked at a railroad station and their car was demolished. Following this, a group of some 60 Skinheads attacked citizens in the center of the city, later escaping aboard a train bound for Prague.

November 1991, Prague. More than a thousand Skinheads and supporters marched for several hours through Wenceslaus Square and then through Zizcov, a largely Gypsy neighborhood, shouting "Gypsies to the gas chambers!"

February 6, 1993, Pilsen. Some 15 or so Skinheads attacked a dozen Bulgarian tourists with clubs, brass knuckles and tear gas at the railway station in Pilsen. Several of the tourists were injured, including a man and a woman who were hospitalized with concussions. The Czech news agency reported the arrest of the youths, who ranged in age from 14 to 18. All were released to their parents.

More recently, on the weekend of March 19 and 20, 1994, various Skinhead factions joined with other right-wing demonstrators in Prague and other cities to commemorate Hitler's division of Czechoslovakia 55 years earlier.

Stalking Gypsy Children

Schoolchildren have not been safe from attack. A 12-year-old Gypsy girl told of an assault by Skinheads as she and her friends walked home from school: "They shouted 'Gypsies!' and they started to beat us. One of them pulled a knife...." There have been many such reports of Skins stalking Gypsy children near schools.

In December 1993, the Czech Ministry of Internal Affairs released a report on racial violence in the country, blaming "extremist groups propagating extreme nationalism, fascism, and anti-Semitism," and mentioning among such groups at least 10 different factions of Skinheads including neo-Nazis. At the same time, the Ministry reported that three Gypsies had been killed by Skinheads since 1990. Another authority, however, Ladislav Goral, a Gypsy who is a senior member of the government's Council on Nationalities, disputed the estimate, stating that there were at least twice that many fatalities.

An evaluation by the Institute for Criminology claims that the general populace of the Czech Republic tends to:

> sympathize with anyone who at least verbally, but better "in reality" stands up for their protection.... Thus, for example, members of a group of skinheads are forgiven and ultimately supported by a considerable part of the population, which mistakes their racist, fascist intolerance for the protection of society from criminality.

Miroslav Martinu, whose Skinhead son Ales had been killed in the aforementioned Oporensky brawl in 1991, insisted that the gangs attacking Gypsies were only going after "criminal elements." But a policeman was quoted in the Czech newspaper *Krety* as saying: "If nothing is done quickly about the Skins, they will soon be running around here in SS uniforms. And if there are no Gypsies around, they will find other targets."

Commenting upon violence against Gypsies in the Czech Republic, the 1993 Human Rights Report of the U.S. Department of State noted:

> Newspaper reports often link such violence with Skinhead provocations. Such was certainly the case in incidents in Plzen [Pilsen] and Pisek in the fall, in each of which a young Roma died as a result of Skinhead violence. There are credible reports that police ignore or condone incidents of violence against the Roma, although the Government has denounced such violence.

As elsewhere in Europe, Skinheads in the Czech Republic gravitate towards the far-right political parties, of which there are several. The leading such party is the Republicans, whose leader, Miroslav Sladek, is notorious for his anti-Semitic, anti-Gypsy, racist speeches. The party registered significant gains in the 1992 elections, garnering 600,000 votes and 11 seats in the 200-seat Czech National Council. It jumped from less than one percent in 1990 to over six percent in 1992, and opinion polls since then indicate public support for the party hovering around four to five percent. While in the past Sladek courted the Skinheads, he currently claims not to seek their support. Nonetheless, these gangs find his party's views appealing.

"You too must fight for the white race!"

Bands and Zines

There is an active Skinhead music scene in the Czech Republic. The leading band, Orlik, reportedly sold 120,000 copies of its first LP and has drawn as many as 600 Skinheads to its concerts. Other active bands are Buldok, Valasska Liga, and Kon-Kwista.

The Czech Skinhead movement boasts a number of popular skinzines that are blatantly Nazi in tone and ideas, and that carry advertisements and articles on neo-Nazi groups and causes around the world. The more ambitious ones are *White Warriors* (a Czech-language publication despite its English name), *Stürmer,* and *Fénix,* which is written in English in an attempt to reach an international audience. Some zines regularly publish materials from Tom Metzger's White Aryan Resistance in Fallbrook, California, Gary Lauck's NSDAP-AO in Lincoln, Nebraska, and the SS Action Group in Dearborn, Michigan.

DENMARK

The Skinhead phenomenon came on the Danish scene in the early 1980's, when its young minions were generally referred to as "Grønjakker" ("green jackets," their distinctive military-style attire). Their activity then was centered in Østerbro in the east of Copenhagen, an area where immigrants were moving into apartments that native Danes had difficulty obtaining. "Green jackets" became embroiled in the controversy, engaging in physical assaults and racist harangues. Some of their leaders received stiff jail sentences for these attacks.

Today the Skinheads' numbers are down. They do have a publication, *The Danish National Front,* and many of them are active members of the right-wing Den Danske Forening (Danish Society). Skinheads show up every year on June 5, "Constitution Day," when public meetings take place around the country. In recent years Skins have been employed on these occasions as bodyguards for the right-wing politician Mogens Glistrup.

First Concert

On June 11, 1994, Skins organized Denmark's first Skinhead concert. Held in Gladsaxe, a Copenhagen suburb, the event drew some 300 Skins from Denmark, Sweden and Germany to hear two bands: Bound For Glory, from the United States, and Svastika, from Sweden. Members of the Danish Nazi party, DNSB, were invited to attend, and did so.

Denmark's Skinheads may have met their match (of a sort) in "De Autonome" ("The Autonomous"), a group of "anti-fascist" militants better organized than the Skins and quite willing to employ violence in their cause. These militants have been accused of setting fire to one of the buses used by Skinheads for transportation to the concert at Gladsaxe.

FINLAND

There are Skinhead groups in several Finnish cities — Helsinki, Turku, Tampere, Lahti, Oulu, Pori — with a membership of between 10 and 50 in each.

Asked for a view of Finland's Skinhead scene in 1992, a member of the Finnish Skin band Mistreat spoke of "a relatively strong scene" in the major cities, "at least a few hundred people who are real Skinheads and many more with a similar attitude."

On the 12th of November, 1992, police arrested a small group of Skinheads for smashing the windows of the Jewish synagogue in Turku. A year later a Finnish Skinhead was quoted in the British skinzine *Last Chance* bragging that Skinheads had attacked refugee centers in Helsinki and in Tampere, and that the movement had "gathered new members fast."

In Helsinki, a Skinhead group fired the editor of its magazine, *Skullhead-Skinhead,* for having written articles condemning Nazi crimes against humanity. As of late 1993, there were skinzines published in at least two Finnish cities, Pori and Vantaa.

FRANCE

Journalists and other observers in France put the number of Skinheads today at 500, down sharply from a high of 1,000 to 1,500 in 1985-86. At the same time, a growing segment of soccer hooligans, aged 15 to 25, appear to have mixed with the Skinheads and to have been influenced by neo-Nazi Skinhead themes. They are known as "casuals," and may include some Skinheads who have shed traditional Skinhead dress and hairstyle.

Skinheads have attacked North African Frenchmen, desecrated Jewish cemeteries, and assaulted journalists covering a right-wing festival. They have joined with non-Skinhead soccer hooligans to assault fans of North African descent at matches, provoked violent clashes with the police, and scuffled with other far-right groups at demonstrations. Some adult extremists on the right have attempted to recruit Skinheads, meeting with short- lived success. Major population centers — the Paris region, Lyons, Lille-Arras, Marseilles — have the largest concentration of Skinheads, who collect in bands of 30 to 40. There have been smaller groups in Le Havre, Angers, Toulouse, Perpignan and Brest.

The ideological themes of French Skinheads include glorification of the white race and hatred for Jews, Arabs, North Africans, Freemasons, capitalism and communism.

White Rebel

Le Rebelle Blanc (The White Rebel) appears to be the organ of the Jeunesses nationalistes révolutionnaires (JNR, Nationalist Revolutionary

Youth), founded by one "Batskin" (true name: Serge Ayoub), after he broke with the far-right Troisième Voie (Third Way), led by Jean-Gilles Malliarakis. According to knowledgeable observers, the JNR numbers some 10 members, and the publication is not so much the work of Skinheads as a JNR attempt to influence and recruit Skinheads. (Another publication, *Skin Europa*, attributes to Batskin's circle the following self-portrait: "Drunk, yes. Alcoholic, no.")

Le Rebelle Blanc contains neo-Nazi and Skinhead symbols. One issue carried references to "the struggle against the cosmopolitans," a codeword for Jews, and a cartoon showing figures of Hitler's henchmen gazing horrorstruck at a caricature of a black. A photo of Skins in front of the JNR flag is captioned, "Skinheads: the nightmare of the zulus." The zine also carries advertisements for the German neo-Nazi group, the Free German Workers Party (FAP) in Münster and the German Skinhead band Werwolf.

Dark Side

Skinzines and Skinhead paraphernalia have been sold at two shops in Paris: Dark Side (the name is in English), in the 14th *arrondissement,* and London Styl in the 18th. Dark Side is said to be the creation of the JNR'S Batskin. The shop was bombed in late 1993 and subsequently reopened in the 15th *arrondissement* under the name Dark Lord. A U.S.-based skinzine breathlessly describes a compact disc sold through Dark Lord as a "must have": in addition to music by French Skinhead bands, the recording has a spoken introduction by Léon Degrelle, the Belgian Waffen SS general who died in Spain March 31, 1994.

A French zine called *Le Côté Obscur* (The Dark Side) appeals to Skinheads, casuals and other soccer hooligans. One issue contains a full-page ad for Batskin's Dark Side shop, and, given the name, is probably linked to him. Each page is bordered by a sort of Greek key design made of swastikas. Cartoons feature riot police fleeing before a hail of bottles, and Skinheads and hooligans beating people with baseball bats. One page features a score system awarding points for running down Arabs: two points for hitting a single Arab, six for a couple, three for a pregnant Arab, four for a woman with a stroller, and a medal for driving into a mosque during prayers. There are also references to the "Judaized media" ("media enjuivées").

Organization

Skinheads appeared in France around 1980. By 1984, they had split into two groups: neo-Nazis, and non-politicals, who were chiefly interested in the music. The latter, who included some black Skinheads, eventually drifted back into society.

Neo-Nazi Skinheads became targets for beatings by suburban black gangs (the Skins' dress and hairstyle having made it easy to identify them). This may have contributed to the precipitous decline in the Skinheads' numbers, and the rise of their successors, the casuals, whose numbers roughly equal the Skinheads. There appears to be some overlap between the Skinheads and the casuals.

The casuals use rabid support for their soccer teams as an excuse for violence and extreme nationalism, sometimes veering into neo-Nazism. Observers describe them as "little whites," who are outnumbered by African or Arab immigrants in their housing projects, mainly located in the suburbs rather than within the limits of large cities. They vent their resentments by giving Nazi salutes and chanting "Sieg Heil!" at soccer matches, where they deface the stands with swastikas and anti-immigrant graffiti and assault the police and other spectators.

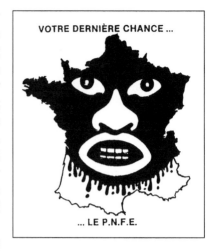

"Your last chance...the PNFE."

Some of the individuals in the stands frequented by Skinheads, casuals, and "hools" (hooligans) identify themselves as members of Jean-Marie Le Pen's Front National; others distribute fliers from the white supremacist Parti Nationaliste Français et Européen (PNFE); still others say they come to soak up the atmosphere and revel in the camaraderie.

Crimes

In September 1993, Skinheads in Paris doused with gasoline and set fire to two young Frenchmen of North African descent, at whom they yelled racist insults. The victims, who suffered burns mostly on their faces and hands, were expected to recover.

In January 1993, two Skinheads who had desecrated a Jewish cemetery in Lyons four months earlier were sentenced to eight months in prison. The pair had been drinking heavily after watching a soccer match. They later broke gravestones in the city's Jewish cemetery and daubed them with slogans such as "Adolf Hitler is our father" and "Death to the Jews."

In the fall of 1993, there were serious incidents at the Paris soccer stadium, the Parc des Princes, during a game between Paris-St. Germain (PSG) and a visiting team. Riot police were driven out of the Kop de Boulogne enclosed stands where Skinheads, casuals and PSG hooligans congregate. A dozen police officers and a police commissioner were injured. The perpetrators appeared to be the Skinheads' putative successors, the casuals.

During the Front National's 1995 St. Joan of Arc's Day parade, held in Paris on May 1, a 29-year-old Moroccan immigrant was murdered by drowning. Witnesses told police that three Skinheads broke away from the parade and hurled insults at Brahim Bouarram before one of the Skins threw him into the Seine. The Front National denied any link to the killing. A Skinhead, Mickael Freminet, 19, reportedly has confessed to pushing Bouarram, but said he did not intend to kill him.

Foreign Links

There are reports of links between French and Belgian Skinheads. French Skinheads have been interviewed by British skinzines. Some French skinzines carry advertisements for German and American Skinhead bands. Still, French Skinheads tend to be ultra-nationalist, and are less eager than their foreign counterparts to forge close ties with Skins in other lands.

Music

The French Skinhead music scene is limited because bands are unable to rent space on account of their record of violence.

Skinheads Pour Eternité (S.P.E.) was a skinzine in Gentilly which folded in late 1991, after five years of publication. However, it has continued distributing records, tapes and magazines and has started releasing records on its own label.

French Skinhead bands have included Force de Frappe (a name taken from the term for the French nuclear force), Kontingent 88, Légion 88 (88 stands for "Heil Hitler," H being the eighth letter of the alphabet), Brutal Combat, Plastic Gangsters, Evil Skins, Guitar Gangster and Urban Gones (both from Lyons), and Viking (from Le Havre). The ideology of some of these bands is unclear; not all are necessarily neo-Nazi.

Record labels include S.P.E., Lion Records, Bird Records, Rebelles Européens, and Bulldog Service. Rebelles Européens, of Brest, has been headed by Gaël Bodilis and Brigitte Maljak, who was a law student in the early 1990's. Both were active in the Front National Jeunesse (the youth wing of Le Pen's movement), and Bodilis in the Troisième Voie as well. Among the label's offerings are titles by the English Skinhead band No Remorse, with record jackets emblazoned with swastikas and portraits of Adolf Hitler. According to the Paris newspaper *Le Monde*, Rebelles Européens was dissolved at the end of 1988, but quietly revived itself in July 1991 with Maljak as president and Bodilis as treasurer. After resuming operations, the firm was very active in producing openly neo-Nazi recordings. During 1995, however, it has shown no signs of functioning.

The French police have actively monitored and countered the Skinheads with arrests, prosecution, and exposure. The Renseignements Généraux (police intelligence division) has applied a strategy of exposure in which information is shared with journalists. Some observers believe timely and effective law enforcement has successfully contained the French Skinhead movement.

GERMANY

The violence that erupted in Germany over the past several years brought to public attention the neo-Nazi Skinheads, a group previously regarded as only a fringe segment of the youth scene. Operating as loosely knit gangs of juvenile thugs, their menacing presence has been noted in communities throughout the recently united country. They have swelled the ranks of right-wing street demonstrators, acted as security guards for neo-Nazi meetings and served as a ready reservoir for extremist agitators to tap for attacks on so-called aliens in German society. From the riotous assaults on foreigners in Hoyerswerda in 1991 to the waves of firebombings and beatings that have followed to this day, the Skinheads have been the main attack dogs.

Molotov Cocktails

September 17, 1991 — Skinheads armed with clubs, rocks and Molotov cocktails attacked a building in Hoyerswerda, an eastern city that housed about 150 foreigners, mostly from Vietnam and Mozambique. Hundreds of local residents gathered to cheer the Skinheads and resist attempts by the police to quell the rampage. The assault and public demonstrations of support continued for days, ultimately ending on September 23, with the evacuation of the besieged housing unit.

August 22-28, 1992 — Rostock, in eastern Germany, was the scene of several nights of Skinhead violence against a hostel housing 200 asylum seekers (mainly Gypsies) and 150 Vietnamese guest workers. The hostel was partially destroyed by the 150 attacking Skinheads, who were openly encouraged by at least 500 cheering local residents. Authorities evacuated the asylum seekers on August 24, and the guest workers fled as the building was being torched. Once again, violence rewarded the Skinheads with victory; the Interior Minister of Mecklenburg-Western Pomerania, the state in which Rostock is located, was subsequently dismissed for having failed to immediately order the police to quell the riot.

November 13, 1992 — Two Skinheads in Wuppertal (in the state of North Rhine-Westphalia) kicked and burned to death a man they mistakenly thought was Jewish, after the owner of the bar in which the victim and perpetrators were drinking shouted, "Jew! You must go to Auschwitz. Auschwitz must reopen! Jews must burn!" The Skinheads kicked the victim until he lost consciousness, poured schnapps on him and set him on fire. He died of internal injuries while the Skinheads drove to the Netherlands in the victim's car, where they dumped the body. In February 1994, the two Skinheads and the bar owner were convicted of murder and given sentences of 14, 8 and 10 years, respectively.

Child Killing

November 23, 1992 — Two Skinheads, aged 19 and 25, firebombed two houses in Mölln, Schleswig-Holstein, killing a Turkish woman, her 10-year-old granddaughter, and 14-year-old niece. Several others were severely injured. The perpetrators telephoned the police station and announced, "There's fire in the Ratzeburger Strasse. Heil Hitler!" They made an identical call to the fire brigade regarding the second address. Michael Peters and Lars Christiansen were tried and convicted in December 1993, and sentenced to life imprisonment, and 10 years, respectively.*

May 29, 1993 — Four Skinheads were charged with setting fire to a home in Solingen, North Rhine-Westphalia, killing five Turkish citizens. Three girls, aged 4, 9 and 12, and an 18-year-old woman, died in the flames. Another victim, a 27-year-old woman, died of injuries suffered when she leaped from a window. Ten others were injured. Neighbors reported hearing the arsonists shout, "Heil Hitler!" The Skinheads were indicted for murder, attempted murder, and arson. Their trial began in April 1994 and was expected to continue for many months.

October 29, 1993 — A group of Skinheads chanting, "Nigger out!" attacked members of the American Olympic luge team training in Oberhof, Thuringia, after a confrontation in a nearby discotheque. Two of the attackers

were convicted in January 1994. One was sentenced to one year, the other to two years and eight months. A third was placed on probation for two years.

March 25, 1994 — A synagogue was firebombed in the northern port city of Lübeck. No injuries were reported, but the synagogue was badly damaged. Four right-wing extremists, ranging in age from 19 to 24, were placed under arrest. While three of them were found guilty of arson and the fourth of complicity in the fire-bombing, they were acquitted of attempted murder even though people were in the synagogue at the time. They were given sentences ranging from two and a half to four and a half years. (Arsonists again attacked the Lübeck synagogue on the night of May 6, 1995, even as elsewhere commemorations of the 50th anniversary of the Nazi surrender in World War II were beginning. Among the ceremonies was a rededication in Berlin—attended by more than 2,000 people, including German Chancellor Helmut Kohl—of a major synagogue destroyed during the war.)

May 12, 1994 — A mob of about 150 youths rampaged against foreigners in Magdeburg, an eastern German city. They beat five Africans on a down-

---

* Around the time of Mölln, large numbers of Germans took to the streets to express outrage at the neo-Nazi violence. In Berlin, a government-backed rally drew 300,000 anti-Nazi protesters, while additional candlelight vigils and protest marches attracted large numbers of Berliners. There followed demonstrations of 400,000 in Munich, 120,000 each in Karlsruhe and Stuttgart, 400,000 in Hamburg, 250,000 in Essen and 200,000 once again in Berlin. It is estimated that a total of some three million Germans took part in these anti-Nazi expressions.

town street and then chased them into a Turkish-owned cafe where four of the assailants were stabbed by cafe employees. Forty-nine rioters — described by police as drunken hooligans and Skinheads — were arrested and released in a few hours. Officials said they were not sure they had enough evidence to bring charges. Four days later charges were finally brought against a 19-year-old, identified as a ringleader of the riot and head of a local neo-Nazi group of about 80 members. Commenting on this event, Germany's then-President Richard von Weizsäcker said: "It is hard to understand how, as we see from television pictures, hoodlums or right-wing extremists can charge through the streets, breaking windows and attacking people, and then 50 or more are arrested, but that same night they're all released." Eventually, a number of additional suspects were prosecuted; nine were sentenced to prison or juvenile terms ranging from 14 months to three and a half years.

July 23, 1994 — Twenty-two neo-Nazi Skinheads desecrated the memorial grounds at the site of the former Buchenwald concentration camp. Arriving by bus from the nearby towns of Erfurt and Gera, the Skinheads ran wild, throwing stones and chanting Nazi slogans. They threatened to set on fire a woman staffer who tried to stop them. When the police arrived, they interrogated the group and released all but one. Criticizing this tepid police response, Ignatz Bubis, the chairman of the Central Council of Jews in Germany, said: "The way the authorities have handled this case and others is an open invitation to repeat the vandalism." Two of the police officials were subsequently suspended, three others were scheduled for disciplinary action, and the rampaging youths were re-arrested. In October, the leader of the Skinhead gang was sentenced to 20 months in jail and five others, all minors, received suspended sentences or fines.

September 1994 — Sachsenhausen, the former Nazi concentration camp in Oranienburg, has been repeatedly vandalized. The camp is maintained as a memorial to the victims of Nazi barbarism. Four Skinheads were caught there on September 2 shouting Nazi slogans. Earlier, guards found Nazi swastikas painted on camp property. On September 4, the unused bakery on the campsite burned down. Previously, a hut containing an exhibit about the Holocaust was destroyed.

Passengers Assaulted

These are among the more dramatic events that have been reported with shock and horror, but numerous other acts of violence have occurred and — at a lesser pace — continue to take place to this day: assaults on individuals, brawls in youth centers, attacks on homes and businesses. For example, in October 1994, a gang of some 20 Skinheads boarded a streetcar in Berlin and severely assaulted passengers they believed were foreigners. The following month, police in Hanau, near Frankfurt, broke up a Skinhead gang of 20 who were suspected of attacking foreigners, a handicapped person and a former synagogue. Seized by police in their raid on the gang were guns, ammunition and banned Nazi propaganda. Two of those arrested were suspected of manufacturing homemade bombs. The gang had links to banned neo-Nazi organizations including the Viking Youth.

According to the Federal Office for the Protection of the Constitution (Bundesamt für Verfassungsschutz), the number of violent right-wing extremists in 1993 was about 5,600, many of them Skinheads. This was a decline from the 1992 estimate of 6,400. In 1993, Skinheads also constituted a large proportion of those who perpetrated 2,232 acts of right-wing violence, including seven homicides and 20 attempted homicides. The comparable 1992 figures were 2,639 violent acts and 18 homicides. The numbers, while showing some improvement, are still shockingly high.

Anti-Jewish Crime

Most of the bigoted violence has been directed against foreigners, especially Turks, but Jews have increasingly become a favorite target. The number of criminal offenses motivated by proven or suspected anti-Semitism in 1994 was 881, an increase of 34 percent over the previous year's figures. Sixty-one of these were acts of violence. (In a separate tally, the German office on crime (BKA) estimated that there were 934 anti-Jewish incidents — 64 of them violent — during 1994.) Although there were 11 fewer anti-Jewish acts of violence in 1994 than in 1993, the total number of criminal acts against Jews in Germany has risen steadily over the past five years, from 208 in 1990 to 656 in 1993 and 881 in 1994. And the perpetrators tend to be young: Fifty-six percent of those suspected of committing violent acts of an extreme-right nature (including attacks against Jews, foreigners and political opponents) were under the age of 21.

The Skinhead lifestyle tends to revolve around gang activities. Criminal citations and jail terms are considered by many to be badges of honor and proofs of courage. Drunken sprees of random violence are routine. "Party until you drop" is the Skinhead jargon for the nightly drinking bouts which often end in the street as the Skins rove in packs looking for victims. "We stand totally drunk in our filth" runs the opening line of a popular Skinhead song by the band Böhse Onkelz (Evil Uncles).* The song celebrates the numbed state of the participants who, even when arrested, continue their "manly" carousing in their cells.

"Doitsche Musik"

The single greatest influence on Skinheads is their music. It bonds them, voices their alienation, and glorifies them as defenders of German honor, while reviling foreigners, Jews, homosexuals, and the left. The lyrics of "Doitsche Musik" (a play on "Deutsche" and "oi") by the band Tonstörung (Sound Disturbance) are graphic:

---

* Böhse Onkelz have since shed their affinity with neo-Nazism.

Sharpen your knife on the sidewalk,
let the knife slip into the Jew's body.
Blood must flow
and we shit on the freedom of this Jew republic...
oiling the guillotine with the Jew's fat.

Until a recent government crackdown, much of the music had an openly Nazi hue, raising up the image of a new storm trooper as the political soldier of the white race. Störkraft (Disturbing Force), one of the most influential of these bands before abandoning neo-Nazism, had applauded the Skinheads as the hard and merciless exemplars of the racial elite:

He is a Skinhead and a fascist
He has a bald head and is a racist
He has no morals and no heart
The features of his face are made of hatred
He loves war and he loves violence
And if you are his enemy, he will kill you.

Another band, Radikahl (word play on "radical" and "bald"), recorded the song "Swastika," whose lyrics call for bestowing on Hitler the Nobel Prize. Volkszorn (People's Wrath) employs as a song title the slogan of Hitler's SA in their street battles, "Rotfront Verrecke" ("Smash the Red Front"). Other bands take their names directly from the National Socialist period: Werwolf, Sturmtrupp, Legion Condor (the German air unit that operated during the Spanish Civil War) and Kraft Durch Froide (an "oi" play on Strength Through Joy — the slogan of the Nazi labor service). At rock concerts, Skinhead crowds whipped into a frenzy often erupt into delirious shouts of "Sieg Heil."

Racist Records

At present, more than 50 Skinhead bands are known to exist in Germany, as well as any number of smaller, amateur groups. Reflecting its subculture status, however, Skinhead music is largely an underground phenomenon. Record and cassette production and sales have mainly been handled through private firms such as Rock-O-Rama, located near Cologne; Skull Records in Bad Überkingen, Baden-Württemberg; and Rebelles Européens in Brest, France. In February 1993, Rock-O-Rama, the largest producer of such recordings, was raided by German police who confiscated about 30,000 CD's, tapes and records. The firm has since been cautious about the materials it handles.

Skinhead concerts are advertised through word of mouth and their locations revealed selectively, in part to prevent disruption by the left or banning by the police.* These concerts sometimes conclude in a rampage, as the

_____

* Most recently, police stopped 231 Skins who were on their way to a concert planned for March 25, 1995, in Triptis (near Erfurt in eastern Germany), and prevented the event from taking place.

Skinheads, flushed with alcohol, run wild. Following one such event in Cottbus, where 600 Skinheads listened to Störkraft, Radikahl, and the visiting British band Skrewdriver, a mini-riot ensued. Drunken revelers spilling out of an open air concert in Massen in October 1992, trashed the stores in the area and assaulted a bus load of Polish tourists. In August 1993, police banned a scheduled concert in Pritzerbe, confiscating a veritable arsenal of weapons from angry Skinheads who had gathered to party and afterwards "flatten a Turk." Shortly before that, some 700 to 900 persons attended a concert in Prieros, Brandenburg, where they heard the German bands Frontal, Brutale Haie, Elbstrum, and the British band Close Shave. In July 1994, still another such concert was attended by 900 right-wing extremists in Rudersdorf, near Berlin.

Until 1989, the "Fascho bands," as they are sometimes called, were confined to West Germany. After the collapse of the repressive Communist regime, a number of east German bands made their appearance. The first major concert was held in Nordhausen in 1990 under the auspices of Torsten Heise of the neo-Nazi group, the Free German Workers Party (FAP).* A year later, fuel was added to the fire when the British band Skrewdriver toured the area encouraging the formation of local bands. One of the first organized was Volkszorn (People's Wrath) in the town of Bruchsal, Baden-Württemberg. Their tape, "Blood and Honor," which likened the Skinheads to the brown shirts, was an instant hit.

Among the most influential Skin bands presently active are: Brutale Haie ("Brutal Sharks" — from Erfurt, Thuringia); Blut und Ehre ("Blood and Honor" — Ludwigsburg, Baden-Württemberg); Endstufe ("Final Stage" — Bremen), Triebtäter ("Rapist" — Mutlangen); Oithanasie (word play on "oi" and "euthanasia" — Gera, Thuringia); Legion Condor (Radevormwald, North Rhine-Westphalia), Landser (East Berlin), Sturmtrupp (Neuberg, Bavaria), Noie Werte (Stuttgart). The bands from the new German states are noted for their particularly brutal, racist and xenophobic songs.

Skinzines

There are at least 60 skinzines in circulation, the majority printed in western Germany. Under names like *Panzerfaust* (a WW II anti-tank weapon), *Shock Troops* and *White Storm*, they offer interviews with Skinhead bands, lists of favorite recordings, song lyrics, poems and cartoons. Inflammatory accounts of street battles and firebombings are printed with the admonition: "The good deeds must go on." A poem, "Hitler's House," published in the Coburg zine *Clockwork Orange*, ends with the words: "Some day the world will realize that Adolf Hitler was right."

Other neo-Nazi skinzines are *Aggressive, Der Patriot, Der Skinhead, Der Sturm* (Storm), *Endsieg* (Final Victory), *Eisenschadel* (Iron Skull), *Erwache* (Wake Up), *Glorreiche Taten* (Glorious Deeds), *Hass und Gewalt* (Hatred and Force), *Heimatfront* (Home Front), *Kahlschlag* (Skin-Blow), *Macht und Ehre* (Might and Honor), *Nahkampf* (Close Combat), *Nordwind* (North Wind), *Proiszens Gloria*

---

* The FAP was banned in February 1995.

(Prussian Glory, misspelled to play on "oi"), *Querschläger* (Ricochet), *Schlachtruf* (Battle Cry), *Unterm Kroiz* (Under the Cross, with a play on "oi"), *White Power*, and *Zeitbombe* (Time Bomb). Also popular in German Skinhead circles is the Swedish publication *Storm,* a virulently anti-Semitic skinzine.

Flux

The zine situation — like the Skin scene in general — is somewhat in flux, a consequence of a crackdown on 12 of them in six states in July 1993. Among staffers taken into custody were Markus Dierchen of *Proiszens Gloria,* Berlin; Carsten Szczepanski of *United Skins,* Brandenburg; Andre Sacher and Angelika Teppich of *Angriff Uslar,* Lower Saxony; Silvia Berisha of *Midgard,* Lower Saxony; Harals Mehr of *Donner Versand,* North Rhine-Westphalia; Ilias Zaprasis of *Anhalt Attacke,* Saxony-Anhalt; and Marco Callies of *Schlagstock,* Schleswig-Holstein.

Ironically, one of the strongest influences on the German Skinhead scene is the American racist movement. English phrases like "White Power" and "White Aryan Resistance" (WAR) are a part of the German Skins' vocabulary. The Confederate flag and Ku Klux Klan imagery are also popular, although attempts to organize the Klan in Germany have met with a feeble response. The most influential American source of hate literature is Gary Lauck's

Nebraska-based NSDAP-AO (National Socialist German Workers Party-Overseas Organization). Particularly popular among Skinheads are his swastika stickers with racist anti-foreigner slogans. British bands and zines are also influential among the German Skins.

Revisionist pamphlets denouncing the Holocaust as a fraud are eagerly read by Skinheads. Two such tracts are "The Leuchter Report," distributed by Ernst Zündel from Canada, and "The Auschwitz Myth," by Wilhelm Stäglich, which claims the Nazi death camps were a Zionist invention.

Anti-Semitism is a staple item in Skinhead circles, with attacks mainly centered on Jewish cemeteries and memorial sites. There has also been an increase in assaults on synagogues. On September 21, 1992, three Skinheads and a known neo-Nazi, Thomas Dienel, carried two halves of a pig's head into the synagogue in Erfurt, along with a death-threatening letter. (Dienel, head of the 600-member German National Party (DNP), was arrested and sentenced to two years and eight months imprisonment.) In March 1994 and May 1995, the aforementioned arsons of a synagogue in Lübeck took place.

Links with Other Neo-Nazis

As early as 1982, one of the first skinzines to appear in Berlin, *Attack,* undertook "as a sacred duty" to convert the Skinhead scene into a disciplined, ideological movement. "The political consciousness of the Skinhead ranges from extremism to anarchy," the magazine noted, "but for most, the only thing is to have a good time." This attitude stymied recruitment by the established neo-Nazi organizations and extremist parties. Despite repeated efforts to attract the Skinheads to their ranks, results were meager at first. The Free German Workers Party (FAP) financed one skinzine, *Querschläger,* and exerted strong influence on another, *White Power,* which first appeared in November 1990. *Clockwork Orange,* one of the most popular skinzines, was published by Ulrich Grossman of Coburg, who, from the mid-eighties on, was a member of the German National Democratic Party (NPD). *Endsieg* (Final Victory) boosted the neo-Nazi brawlers of the now-banned Nationalist Front (NF), as did the magazine *The New Day,* which printed the "action program" of the NF in one issue. Another example is the case of the neo-Nazi Dieter Riefling, whose zine *The Activist* promoted the FAP and the Relief Agency for National Political Prisoners and their Dependents (HNG).

The one-time manager of the band Volkszorn, Andreas Gängel, was active in the Nationalist Front, and until June 1992 disseminated the zine *Endsieg.* A local Skin band, the Groilmeiers, has been composed of FAP members. According to *Informationsdienst* (a monthly intelligence newsletter on terrorism, extremism and organized crime), the former drummer for the Kraft Durch Froide band, Andreas Siegfried Pohl, was chief of the organizing department of the NF, and was active behind the scenes in the neo-Nazi Society for the Advancement of Middle German Youth (FMJ), which was banned in 1993. In Autumn 1993 the group renamed itself Direkte Aktion/Mitteldeutschland. Its publication *Der Angriff* (Attack), whose title is taken from the newspaper of Hitler's chief propagandist, Joseph Goebbels, has since 1993 stood out for its advocacy of aggressive xenophobia, anti-Semitism, and violence. "Nobody can tell us," said *Der Angriff's* issue no. 5 (Winter 1994), "that he was not pleased when things started in Rostock" (referring to the burning down of a refugee hostel in August 1992). The same issue denounced reformed Skin bands, such as Störkraft, which distanced itself from xenophobic killings with its song "Arson Murderers — you don't belong to us." *Der Angriff's* preference is the aforementioned band Brutale Haie, which it calls "honest." Direkte Aktion is oriented toward the recruitment of unemployed and disoriented youth in the new German states. In January 1994 the police conducted pre-dawn raids on the group's hangouts in five states, and Brandenburg authorities banned the organization in May 1995.

The more established right-wing parties are of less interest to the Skinheads. Franz Schönhuber's party, Die Republikaner, officially discourages Skinhead participation. (How the Skins cast their secret ballots at election time is, of course, another matter.) Gerhard Frey's German Peoples Union (DVU), and the German National Democratic Party (NPD), while stoking the fire with their nationalist and anti-foreigner rhetoric, publicly keep their distance. Their public posture notwithstanding, one of the individuals charged in the murderous anti-foreigner arson in Solingen has been identified in press accounts as having been a member of the DVU. In Mülheim, North Rhine-Westphalia, a 56-year-old Turk died of a heart attack after having been assaulted on March 9, 1993, by two 21-year-old Skinhead types. The two, both of whom had criminal records and were members of the Republikaner Party, first verbally insulted the victim with the epithet "Shit-Turk" and similar phrases. They then pushed him to the ground, and one of them pointed a gas pistol at the victim's head and pulled the trigger three times. Although the pistol misfired, the victim was so frightened that his heart collapsed. The assailants got four years in prison, and the Republikaner Party says it expelled them. There have also been cases of NPD members participating in xenophobic crimes like arson against the homes of foreigners.

Unity and Struggle

These cases, however, remain the exception so far. For one thing, tactical reasons discourage the election-oriented parties from favoring direct affiliation with Skinheads; for another, most Skins have a distaste for these parties which they see as part of "the system." Yet the situation remains somewhat fluid. An example is the youth organization of the NPD, the Junge Nationaldemokraten (JN), which has around 150 activists. This group has lately adopted a militant approach, and disregarded official NPD policy prohibiting contacts with neo-Nazi groups. Last year *Einheit und Kampf* (Unity and Struggle), the organ of the JN, published an interview with Andreas Siegfried Pohl, a former member of a Skin band, who was an official of the banned Nationalist Front. In the interview Pohl called for a "youth" and "youth-style" (read: "Skinhead") role in "redeveloping a national APO," or extra-parliamentary opposition, a codeword suggesting street fighters. The January 1994 issue of *Einheit und Kampf* advertised concerts featuring the aforementioned hardline Skin bands Brutale Haie, Frontal, Triebtäter, and Noie Werte, organized "in cooperation with" the JN. Another ad in the paper sought a new producer for the Brutale Haie band.

There is also evidence that convicted Skinheads are receiving a thorough indoctrination in neo-Nazi ideology at "comradeship evenings" held in prison. Particularly active on this front is the aforementioned Relief Agency for National Political Prisoners and their Dependents, a right-wing group that sends a steady stream of propaganda to incarcerated neo-Nazi radicals and Skinheads.

Germany's Skinheads have also developed a growing network of contacts with Skinheads in other European countries, notably England, France, Holland, Sweden, Austria, Hungary and, to some degree, Poland.

Eastern Factor

The collapse of the Communist regime in East Germany significantly affected the Skinhead situation. The emergence of the eastern Skins radicalized the Skinhead scene in both numbers and militancy. The aforementioned annual reports of the German intelligence services placed the total number of militant right-wing extremists (the majority of them Skinheads) at 6,400 in 1992 (2,600 in the west, 3,800 in the new eastern states) and

5,600 in 1993 (3,000 in the west and 2,600 in the east). Taking population figures into account, these estimates show a disproportionately high Skinhead presence in the new states.

Among the principal beneficiaries of the radicalization was the FAP, with a spillover membership in Michael Swierczek's National Offensive, Frank Hübner's German Alternative, Christian Worch's National List, and the Nationalist Front; all have subsequently been banned. The latter four were youth-oriented groups that emphasized street marches and "direct action." The Hamburg-based National List was banned by Hamburg authorities, and the others by federal officials.

Another group recently outlawed was the Viking Youth, a neo-Nazi organization with about 400 young members. Members of the organization have in recent years associated with the Skinheads. Federal Interior Minister Manfred Kanther announced the ban in early November 1994, saying there was no place in Germany for "groups like the Viking Youth that propagate racism and anti-Semitism and teach youths to be violent, intolerant and to hate democracy."

While slow at first to counter the neo-Nazi menace of recent years, the German government has since demonstrated increasing vigor in dealing with the problem. Utilizing the tools available to it under the postwar German Constitution, it has banned some neo-Nazi groups, confiscated their propaganda materials and arrested many (including Skinheads) who have broken the law. The controversial constitutional change adopted in 1993, limiting the flow of refugees into the country, has moderated the anti-foreigner fever that earlier gripped the land.

The consequence has been a gradual decline in the strength and rate of crime of Skinheads and other right-wing extremists. At the same time, the far-right political parties — the Republikaners and the DVU — have fared poorly in the recent federal elections.

A Real Threat

These positive trends notwithstanding, the extremist threat to German democracy has not gone away. Particularly disturbing are the rising numbers of anti-Semitic crimes, a trend which seems to indicate that Jews, as distinct from other "foreigners," are coming to be regarded by some German right-extremists as the "main enemy." Furthermore, segments of the neo-Nazi movement in Germany are believed to be accumulating weapons and going underground. Sources report that internal neo-Nazi discussions revolve around the idea of "armed resistance."

Finally, the earlier profile of the German Skinhead as poorly educated, unemployed, and the product of a broken home must, in the light of later research, be revised. Police statistics now reveal a different — and more disturbing — picture. An evaluation (1991-1993) of almost 500 militant right-wing extremists (particularly Skinheads) arrested for violent actions showed 33.6% pupils, students and apprentices; 28.7% skilled workers and craftsmen; 11.3% unskilled workers; 5.6% office workers; 7.9% soldiers — and only 11.3% unemployed. Thus, these violent extremists have been coming in substantial measure from the middle ranges of society, not just the "lumpen" fringe.

HUNGARY

In Hungary, the animating fire of Skinheads is the naming of enemies. Here "enemies" refers — more than to any other group—to the Roma (Gypsies). But the term is used for others as well: foreign students and guest workers, Arabs, blacks, Cubans, homosexuals, liberals, the poor, the homeless and, of course, Jews.

When the Skinhead movement first arose in Hungary in the early 1980's, it was a small but vocal force among those opposed to the then-Communist regime. When that regime fell, the restless animus of the Skinheads turned toward the Gypsy population and the growing numbers of "non-Hungarians" (sometimes including Jews, but more particularly "non-Whites") whom they regarded as dangerous criminal elements. There are presently a few thousand non-white aliens in Hungary, most of them students. (A large number of them have left the country during the past couple of years, with insults and danger cited as major reasons.) The Skinheads have proclaimed that physical attacks are the only effective means of driving the strangers back to their native lands.

Arrow-Cross

Skinhead "ideals" include nationalism, irredentism (the establishment of "Greater" Hungary with widened frontiers) and a purifying of the populace through the eventual elimination of the aforementioned enemies. Some Skinheads openly profess Nazi ideals and have sported the Nazi swastika and the arrow-cross badge worn by Hungarian fascists during World War II; others reject that image. (In April 1993 Hungary's parliament outlawed both the arrow-cross symbol and the swastika.)

Responsible sources estimate the number of Skinheads in Hungary to be between 4,500 and 5,000. About half of Hungary's Skinheads are in Budapest, with other concentrations in Eger, Miskolc and Szeged. There are Skinhead groups in at least 13 of Hungary's 19 counties.

The Hungarian Skins began to organize on a national level in 1990 when they held their first national conclave in Eger. Certain international linkages were forged that year — e.g., with German rightists including the ideologue Gerhard Frey, leader of the German Peoples Union (DVU). The journal

of a neo-fascist segment of Hungarian Skinheads, *Kitartás* (Holding Out), has been published since 1990 by Frey's group in Germany. Two other Skinhead journals were launched that year: *Pannon Bulldog* and *Árpád Népe*. Subsequently, the American neo-Nazi Gary Lauck of Nebraska began publishing *Új Rend* (New Order) in Hungarian for an openly neo-Nazi Skinhead faction. Hungarian Skinheads have ties with Austrian, Italian, Polish, Czech and American organizations, as well as the World Community of Anti-Communist Hungarians, headquartered in Australia.

One of Hungary's more active and extreme groups with Skinhead membership is the Szálasi Guards, named in honor of Ferenc Szálasi, Hungary's Nazi leader in World War II who was executed as a war criminal. It is headed by a youth known only — and proudly — as "Mengele," after the infamous doctor at Auschwitz. Mengele reportedly puts the Guards' membership at "a few dozen." These members have been known to attack Gypsies, Arabs, Jews and foreigners in the streets. Mengele acknowledged his group's responsibility for a bomb threat against a Budapest synagogue early in 1994. "We wanted them" (the Jews), he told a newspaper, "to realize that times are changing and that there are such organizations that do not like the open Semite lunge in the Parliament. We want them to notice that we are here."

Among other extreme-right groups with Skinhead followings are the Hungarian National Frontline (MNA), headed by István Györkös, whose newspaper is the one published by the American neo-Nazi Lauck; the World National Popular Rule Party (VNP) led by Albert Szabó, who describes Hitler's onetime Hungarian leader Szálasi as "one of our models"; and the Hungarian National Movement, headed by László Romhányi, who is in prison for his part in the torture and murder of a homeless man. Szabó's group was the target of a recent police raid. Also active are the Pannon Skinheads, the Roys, and a group called Új Rend (New Order) which is not connected with Gary Lauck's newspaper of the same name.

Hangouts

The Hungarian Skins hang out in discos and beer halls. Their haunts in Budapest include the Viking club, Petőfi Csarnok disco, Öcsi wine bar, Steffl beer-house, Izsák wine bar, Ketlen disco, Fekete Lyuk (Black Hole) club, Total car club, and Kéknyelű wine bar. They can often be found hanging around major thoroughfares in Budapest. In Eger, the best known restaurants frequented by Skinheads are Taverna and Express.

The weapons Skinheads have been known to carry include baseball bats, chains, knives, iron rods, chair legs, etc. Like their foreign counterparts they often wear the heavy Doc Martens boots.

Skins are active in rifle clubs, sports clubs, and at military secondary schools (a major Skinhead base is in the military academy in Eger). They are not "lumpens." Most come from families of professionals and have at least an eighth grade education.

As elsewhere, music is a major part of the Skinhead scene. Typical are the "oi" sounds of the English Skin bands, a particular favorite among them being Skrewdriver. The leading Hungarian bands during the early period (the mid-1980's) were Mos-Oi, Közellenség (Public Enemy), and Oi-Kor, the latter still staging concerts in the 1990's. Mos-Oi has since changed its name to Pannon Skins. Among the newer bands are Archivum, which once played at the headquarters of the Smallholders Party; Magozott Cseresznye (Pitted Cherry), which plays at the Viking Club in Budapest; and today's most popular band, Egészséges Fejbőr (Healthy Skinhead).

A favorite Skinhead song for some years now has been "Gypsy-Free Zone," written by members of the Mos-Oi band:

> We will do away with everything bad;
> Everything base and evil will disappear;
> A blazing gun is the
> Only weapon I can win with.
> I will kill every Gypsy, adult or child...
> When the job is done, we can post
> [the sign] "Gypsy-free Zone."

Mayhem became more than a song or a mere boast as the Skins grew to become a national menace in the early 1990's. Hungary's Office of National Security reported 25 Skinhead assaults in Budapest alone in 1991. Nationally, the Martin Luther King Association, which records attacks on foreign students, reported complaints in 70 instances, with 53 persons listed in police records as attack victims. The MLK Association listed 63 victims during the first half of 1992. In November of that year, a 32-year-old Gypsy man, Zoltán Danyi, was beaten to death by two 15-year-old Skinheads. On August 30, 1992, a national holiday, Skinheads who gathered in the center of the city of Eger shouted Nazi slogans and beat up a passerby thought to be Jewish.

President Shouted Down

On October 23, 1992, the 36th anniversary of Hungary's 1956 anti-Soviet revolt, hundreds of Skinheads, marching into Budapest in their boots and bomber jackets and openly carrying Nazi symbols, shouted down President Árpád Göncz, preventing his delivery of a patriotic speech. (The role of the police in this event has been called into question.)

Hungary's police have generally been less than vigilant in their attention to Skinhead lawlessness, at times even ignoring street assaults against Gypsies. In part, the problem appears to stem from an underlying sympathy of some police officers with Skinhead prejudices. The Skinheads themselves, formerly hostile toward the police, have for tactical reasons adopted a more friendly stance.

Skins in Budapest have a doting elder in István Porubszky, a painter who fled the country after the 1956 revolt and now heads a "1956 Anti-Fascist and Anti-Bolshevik Association" which trains Skinheads in right-wing philosophy. Porubszky hopes to register his trainees as a political party.

"Sixteen-year-olds cannot change anything if the Government will not allow it," said a Budapest youngster whose Skinhead boyfriend was sentenced to a year in prison, "but when our generation comes to power, the country will be run according to our principles." And at a "national congress" of Skinheads held in Budapest in November 1992, its organizer, István Szőke, was quoted as saying: "As much blood needs to flow for the Fatherland as is necessary. Either there will be radical changes or anything may happen."

Later that month a long, major trial of 48 Skinheads ended, with all convicted of causing severe bodily injuries and disturbing the public order by their unprovoked attacks on Africans, Arabs and Gypsies. Nine were given prison sentences and the remaining 39 were placed on parole.

In January 1993, five Skinheads assaulted a young Jewish woman, stabbed her in the stomach and carved a swastika on her breast. It appeared that the woman had been followed for some time before the attack. The atrocity was the subject of debate in the Parliament, where a member, Izabella Király, called the attackers "good sons of the Hungarian nation." That same month, Budapest police arrested eight Skinheads for assaulting people aboard a trolley car; a search of the homes of the eight uncovered swastika armbands and literature defaming Jews and foreigners.

Skinheads' "Mother"

A note of optimism sounded a few months later when Hungary's ruling Democratic Forum (MDF) expelled some members of the party's right wing, led by István Csurka, even though it meant losing parliamentary seats. Many of the rightists hold anti-Semitic views. Among those expelled was the aforementioned Izabella Király, who has been nicknamed "Mother of the Skinheads." After her expulsion she created the Hungarian Interest Party (MEP) and continued to be a supporter of the Skinheads and an apologist for their actions.

Skinhead attacks continued in 1994. In March, two Skinheads stabbed a Jewish passenger on a Budapest subway. In November, in the town of Gyöngyös, Skinheads threw Molotov cocktails into a Roma family's home, burning it down. One of the victims of the crime has alleged police misconduct in the handling of the case. According to police, two Skinheads burned two Torah scrolls in a synagogue in the eastern city of Debrecen on January 6, 1995, the birthday of the aforementioned Hungarian Nazi leader Ferenc Szálasi.

At least one police official has been outspoken about the Skinhead problem. Dr. György Gábriel, a detective who heads the Family, Child and Youth Protection division of the Budapest Police Force, has stated that "beginning at the end of 1991, the Skinhead movement began to grow wider, and they began to enter the world of crime. They steal, they murder, they mug.... This," he said, "is a society in crisis. Everything is in crisis: the economy, the family, the school system, the legal system, the police.... We have a high rate of suicide, and now drugs are coming in, it's no wonder that the most sensitive stratum, youth, is reacting this way...."

IRELAND

The neo-Nazi Skinhead movement in Ireland is very small, a circumstance that the Irish Skinheads lament. "We have plenty of nationalists," writes one, "but not enough National Socialists!"

Two groups, the Irish Hammer Skins and Women for Aryan Unity, share a Dublin post office box. An Irish Skinhead band, Celtic Dawn, has recorded an album titled "Europe's Honour," according to the British Skinhead publication *Last Chance*.

ITALY

The Skinhead presence in Italy, set on the historic stage of Fascism, combines the broad patterns of the world neo-Nazi Skinhead movement with the unique qualities of the Italian scene. The "Naziskins" — as Skinheads are known locally — represent the most violent grouping on Italy's far right.

The Interior Ministry has estimated hard-core neo-Nazi Skinhead membership in Italy at something over a thousand and youthful sympathizers or hangers-on at two or three thousand. Virtually all of the known Italian Skinheads participated in a national neo-fascist rally held in 1992 to commemorate the 70th anniversary of the Fascist "March on Rome" that catapulted Mussolini to power. They gathered in Rome's Piazza Venezia beneath the balcony from which Mussolini used to mesmerize crowds.

The various Italian Skinhead groups constitute a force that is able to exploit resentments prevalent among young people (e.g., the growing anger towards immigrants in Italian cities). And while anti-Semitism is not the chief theme of the Skins, it is undoubtedly present and potentially dangerous.

(Note: In Italy it is difficult — and often impossible — to distinguish between the works of actual Skinheads and those of their violent mimics. The Skins frequently mix with other rowdies — for example, fanatical soccer hooligans who chant anti-Semitic slogans and display Nazi symbols in Italian stadiums. Such fans are not necessarily Skinheads, but many assume the Skinhead style.)

Violence and Bigotry

Skinheads in Italy have assaulted refined-looking students from middle class homes, drug addicts, homosexuals and prostitutes. Their favorite victims are *extracomunitari* — immigrants — from Third World or eastern European countries and the homeless. Persons sleeping in the streets have been set afire on several occasions, and Naziskins in Rome are known to have torched residences of foreigners.

A week of violence by Skins and their imitators: On August 23, 1993, in Riccione, an Adriatic beach resort, seven Skinheads shouting racist slogans beat up a 25-year-old woman from Cameroon. The same night in Sardinia, three youths, also spouting hatred, beat a Moroccan man. A few days earlier, youths attacked a Moroccan family in their house in Rome. That same week in Milan, a group of six teenagers described as coming from "good families," and calling themselves the Anti-Bum Squad, brutally assaulted a homeless man. "Milan has become unlivable," one of the youths was quoted saying. "Seeing that no one has ever been concerned in cleaning things up, we are doing it ourselves."

Similar acts of violence against foreigners continue to take place periodically. In February 1994, five Skins beat and stabbed a Tunisian passenger on a bus; in June, four Skinheads attacked a Muslim religious leader in a small city. In both these incidents, the perpetrators received suspended sentences.

Anti-Semitism

While there have been relatively few physical assaults by Skins against the persons of Jews as such, it is common to see anti-Semitic graffiti with swastikas on the walls of buildings, and Jewish cemeteries have been repeatedly vandalized in Naples, Livorno and other cities. A 20-year-old Palestinian medical student in Rome was beaten up because he had expressed opposition to the campaigns of anti-Jewish hate. In a pamphlet written for a Skinhead rally at San Giuliano Milanese the "Common Enemies" were defined as "blacks, Jews, dirty people" and, of course, *extracomunitari.*

Police called in to quell Skinhead disturbances have themselves come under assault. On April 16, 1995, Skinheads clashed with police in Primavalle, a suburb of Rome. The date marked the twelfth anniversary of an arson attack on the home of a local far-right figure that resulted in the deaths of two of his children. Armed with clubs, Skins gathered at the site of the attack, fought with police and threw stones at cars parked in the area. Three Skinheads were charged with "resistance and aggression against a public official" and 15 others with participating in an unauthorized demonstration and carrying arms without permission. Five policemen required medical attention. That same evening, a group of 10 Skinheads clashed briefly with police in Frascati, also near Rome, before being forced to disperse.

The Mancino Law

In April 1993, the Italian government decreed an emergency measure (Decree No. 122) against "racial, ethnic and religious discrimination"; it was transformed into Law No. 205 two months later. Widely known as the Mancino Law after then-Interior Minister Nicola Mancino, whose signature it bears, the law permits the prosecution of individuals for "incitement to violence," for a broad range of hate crimes that includes the use of symbols of hate. Before the law's passage, prosecutors were limited to charging the perpetrators of hate crimes with specific offenses such as attempted murder, arson or assault — crimes for which convictions are difficult to secure. Hundreds of youths have been convicted under the new law.

More than 60 Italian Skinheads were recently brought to trial in Milan on a range of charges under the Mancino Law. The defendants stand accused, variously, of beating African immigrants and Jews, supporting Nazi ideology, fomenting racial violence, and setting fire to an Anarchist club. Also indicted were Maurizio Boccacci, 38, an organizer of Skinheads, and Dr. Sergio Gozzoli, 65, an outspoken anti-Semite and Holocaust-denier. After the opening session, the trial was scheduled to resume in January 1996.

Skinhead Organizations

Many Skinheads have been organized under the leadership of the Movimento Politico Occidentale (Political Movement of the West), founded by the aforementioned Maurizio Boccacci with headquarters on the Via Domodoscala in Rome and a base in Frascati. It has established ties with far-rightists in Germany, France and Britain. MPO Skins were attacked in November 1992 by young Roman Jews infuriated by the plastering of yellow stars on some 100 Jewish shops in the city. After being banned by the government, the MPO recently renamed itself *I Camerati,* a term used by Mussolini for Fascist party members. In December 1994, Boccacci and nine other extremists were arrested on charges of violence, resisting arrest, and wounding a policeman who was stabbed during clashes at a November soccer match in Brescia.

Skinheads have been particularly active in the Lazio region, with 300 to 500 supporters under the MPO; in Lombardy, with 300 members in Azione Skinhead (Skinhead Action); and in Venetia, with 150 to 300 in the Veneto Fronte Skinhead (Skinhead Front of Venetia). They are divided into groups of about 20 members each, some organized under a federation called Base Autonoma (Autonomous Base).

At the recent national party convention of the neo-fascist Movimento Sociale Italiano (Italian Social Movement), a majority of the delegates voted to dissolve the MSI and merge into the more mainstream Alleanza Nazionale (National Alliance) in an attempt to achieve greater respectability. In addition, a strong statement against anti-Semitism was passed by the assembly. In response, the hard-line minority — Skinheads among them — has split off to re-establish the MSI on the fringe of the far-right political spectrum.

Ideology and Propaganda

Those providing the Skinhead gangs with their propaganda themes and materials include a significant bloc of Italy's veteran right-wing extremists, survivors of an older generation of post-World War II neo-Nazis and Fascists. One name mentioned by Interior Minister Mancino was that of Franco Freda, a publisher of neo-Nazi literature in Padova. Such types have shaped and manipulated the anger of young Skinheads by focusing their attention on well-known hate themes of long standing: (1) "Historical revisionism" — the denial of Nazi genocide against the Jews; (2) hatred or fear of foreigners, based on myths of Aryan racial "purity"; (3) the demonization of Jews in the context of a sinister "plot" to run the world.

Such a conspiracy — if not a Jewish one, then sometimes a plot of the bankers, the Masons, secret government controllers of various loyalties, etc. — is a favorite bugaboo in Skinhead literature under the term *mondialismo* ("globalism"), used to describe a dread planetary system under the control of assorted conspirators.

The style of these dire warnings is typically neo-Nazi. *Azione Skinhead*, from Milan, the one nationally distributed Skinhead zine, reported on a recent Skinhead rally in Rome thus:

> Hundreds of people, hundreds of heads united by a sole ideal, a sole source of pride: the race ... defending our rights, the rights of white Aryans, the rights of Italians. The only ones who can and must combat this planetary system are we.

Two other zines that have circulated in the north are *La Fenice* (The Phoenix) and *Blitz Krieg*.

Naziskin Bands

The Skinhead music scene in Italy is largely based in the northern sector of the country, with the largest concentration of groups in the Venetia region. Here, since 1988, Nazi Skin bands from Germany, France and England have held concerts. The first Skinhead music festival in the south was held in November 1992. Featuring the group Blood and Honour, the festival was watched over by guards in black uniforms with Nazi symbols.

The most popular Skinhead music tapes are those produced by Rock-O-Rama Records, a German firm, though other distributors are also active. Italian lyrics, sung by groups with names such as Peggior Amico (Worst Friend), Gesta Bellica (Martial Feats), Verdi Bianco Rosso (Green White Red: the colors of the Italian flag), Klasse Kriminale (Criminal Class), SS 20, and Powerskins are expressions, variously, of hate, violence and ultranationalism. One band has taken the name A.D.L. 122, short for "Anti-Decreto Legge 122," expressing opposition to the aforementioned government decree against racial, ethnic and religious discrimination.

Peggior Amico, from Vicenza, has been playing since the late eighties and is one of Italy's most well-known and most political racist Skinhead bands. They have played abroad and their records have been acclaimed in English and other foreign skinzines. Songs by SS 20 and Powerskins appear in a compilation tape of Skin bands around the globe called "White Pride World Wide." Skinhead music fan clubs carry such belligerent names as Bulldogs, Gioventu Nazista (Nazi Youth), and Brigata Tafferugli (Fight Brigade). Compact discs featuring old Nazi and Fascist songs are also notable favorites of the Skinheads.

JAPAN

Despite a paucity of hard information, some evidence has come to light of a Skinhead scene in Japan. Its ideological make-up, however, is not clear.

Foreign Skinhead zines have carried reports about Japanese Skinhead music. Among the bands mentioned are Sledgehammer, Bad Vultures, Ouka, Growl Strike, and Gruesome. Their views are not known, although Sledgehammer has been described as a "nationalist" band.

One skinzine suggested that SHARP — Skinheads Against Racial Prejudice — has achieved a following in Japan. It said that SHARP bands "attract a couple of thousand to each gig in comparison to a mere hundred to the right-wing gigs."

LUXEMBOURG

Racist Skinheads and other far-right extremists in Luxembourg are few in number, but they have been responsible for several attacks in recent years.

Following the outbreak of neo-Nazi Skinhead violence in the eastern German town of Hoyerswerda in September 1991, a number of assaults occurred in Luxembourg over the next few months. Two Skinheads beat a man, for no apparent reason, in a pub in Rumelange. In Esch-sur-Alzette, Luxembourg's second-largest city, a Skinhead gave a man a public beating, again for no apparent reason. In another episode, four people paraded through the streets of Rumelange with a Nazi flag, shouting "Heil Hitler," "Sieg Heil" and "Luxembourg to the Luxembourgers." They then tried attacking a residence housing refugees from the former Yugoslavia, and finally they beat a man in the street. The offenders in each case spent several months in jail.

On August 13, 1994, the anniversary of the death of Rudolf Hess, a group of 150 neo-Nazi Skinheads crossed the border from Germany to demonstrate in front of the German embassy in Luxembourg. The police intervened, and within hours the Skins were deposited back at the frontier and told not to return.

A neo-Nazi skinzine called *Das Kroitz* has been produced in the town of Pétange, in southern Luxembourg. (For the newsletter's name, the letters "eu" in the word Kreuz — German for cross — are replaced with "oi.")

The Skinheads' views are shared in Luxembourg's political arena by an extremist party known as the National Bewegung (National Movement). Led by Pierre Peters, the National Bewegung has campaigned on an anti-foreigner platform directed against Portuguese and other foreign workers. The party performed poorly in the most recent elections.

THE NETHERLANDS

The Netherlands' neo-Nazi Skinheads have assaulted and killed perceived enemies. They also dot the ranks of a broader Dutch racist movement; several belong to a small neo-Nazi organization and to two far-right political parties.

After a period of dormancy, the Skinhead movement in the Netherlands has undergone a revival in the last two years. Experts there put the number of Skinheads today at 300 to 600.

The western Netherlands — Rotterdam, the Hague, and Amsterdam — boasts the largest concentration of Skins, with a smaller number in Groningen in the North.

A Skinhead magazine, *Hou Kontakt* (Keep in Touch), has played a role in the Dutch neo-Nazi Skinhead revival. The magazine is published by Martin van der Grind, and can only be obtained by those who can give the name of a known neo-Nazi Skin as a reference. *Hou Kontakt* has articles on Skinhead bands, bars which Skins favor, and runic symbols (with interpretations harking back to those of Hitler's SS). It also carries advertisements for other Skinhead groups, sales outlets for records and tapes, and material from "Oi-stuff," a mail-order house in Utrecht which sells T-shirts and stickers emblazoned with Nazi symbols. The slogans include "Adolf Hitler, our Führer," "Liberate Europe from the Jews," and "In heaven there are no niggers, that's why we molest them here."

Dutch Youth Front

Until 1990 most Dutch neo-Nazi Skins belonged to the Dutch Youth Front (JFN) and the Action Front of National Socialists (ANS), a small neo-Nazi group linked to a banned German organization, Gesinnungsgemeinschaft der Neuen Front (Like-minded Association of the New Front). The ANS is virulently anti-Semitic and has distributed Holocaust-denying propaganda.

After the JFN was banned in 1990, followers switched to the Center Party '86, whose leaders include Tibor Mudde, formerly treasurer of the JFN.

Some Skins are members of the Center Democrats (CD), another far-right party which has three seats in Parliament. CD member Monique Bosman owns the post office box from which "Oi-stuff" sends its catalogs of Nazi wares.

Finally, the Netherlands are not immune from a disturbing trend crossing Europe: soccer hooliganism with an anti-Semitic and neo-Nazi flavor. In November 1992 police arrested 20 people at a soccer match after they broke into anti-Semitic and racist catcalls and made hissing sounds to imitate Nazi gas chambers.

In January 1993 riot police prevented 1,000 fans singing anti-Semitic songs and shouting Nazi slogans from attending a soccer match in an Amsterdam suburb. The visiting team, Ajax of Amsterdam, is regarded as Jewish by many of its own supporters as well as rival fans. Spectators have also shouted racist epithets at black members of the team, thrown bananas and made "jungle" noises.

Such bigotry-tainted hooligans provide fertile ground for Skinheads looking to swell their ranks.

"He Looked Like a Hippie"

The record of violence of Dutch Skinheads began with a May 1982 assault on leftist "squatters" in Amsterdam, to celebrate the victory of a right-wing Parliamentary candidate. Skinheads graduated to murder the following year, when Kerwin Duinmeijer, a 15-year-old black youth from the Netherlands Antilles, was stabbed to death. In 1986 Franky Kattenberg was convicted and jailed for four years for murdering Michael Poye, because "he looked like a hippie." Since then, there have been many Skinhead assaults against "foreigners," blacks and gays. In 1992, assaults were committed in Amsterdam, the Hague, Utrecht, Rotterdam, Leeuwarden, Purmerend and Tilburg.

Eight armed Skinheads were arrested on weapons charges in Arnhem in October 1992. They allegedly intended to disrupt a meeting of an anti-Nazi group, in retaliation for the banning of a Skinhead concert in Rotterdam.

Foreign Links

Dutch Skinheads are linked to hate groups in the United States and Britain through the importation of propaganda materials, and repeated attempts to arrange concerts by British Skinhead bands. The printed material, distributed by the "Oi-stuff" mail order firm, comes from such groups as the various Ku Klux Klans, Gary Lauck's Nebraska-based NSDAP-AO and the British Blood and Honour enterprise.

Music

No Remorse, a British group, first performed in the Netherlands in June 1992. The event drew an audience of 250. Four months later, a concert organized by *Hou Kontakt,* which was to have featured the British groups Squadron and Skullhead, was banned by Dutch authorities. The traffic appears to run in only one direction, since there do not appear to be any Dutch Skinhead bands. As mentioned above, Dutch Skins keep abreast of news on the music front through *Hou Kontakt.* The skinzine also carries advertisements for record and tape outlets.

Finally, although the Skinheads are comparatively modest in number, they may succeed in recruiting among the growing number of soccer hooligans who have a taste for neo-Nazi rhetoric. Regardless of size, Dutch Skinheads pose a threat of violence against a society which, from the end of World War II until recently, had remained remarkably free of serious bigotry-spawned violence. This threat appears to be taken seriously by police authorities and private watchdog groups alike.

NEW ZEALAND

A small racist and anti-Semitic Skinhead movement is known to exist in New Zealand, although estimates of its numbers are difficult to come by. The adult neo-fascist groups that provide the Skins with ideological guidance are themselves believed to have no more than 200 members combined.

One far-right group, the New Zealand National Front, has published a newsletter called *Skinhead*.

Skinhead attacks are rare. Where they have occurred, the victims have tended to be members of the Indian community.

New Zealand's most notorious Skinhead crime took place in October 1989, when Skinhead Glen McAllister went on a shooting spree with a pump action shotgun in Cathedral Square in Christchurch. He killed 22-year-old Wayne Motz, and then shot himself to death. McAllister had been released from jail only a week before the shooting, after having served two years and three months of a four-year sentence for stabbing another Skinhead. At McAllister's burial, several Skinheads, including his brother, Craig, displayed a Nazi flag and gave the stiff-arm Nazi salute.

Recently, there have been reports of at least one prosecution of a Skinhead in Christchurch for violation of the Anti-Racial Vilification Section of the Human Rights Act.

NORWAY

The Norwegian Skinhead movement is young and rather small, probably numbering some 100 to 150. Not all of them fit the neo-Nazi label. In addition to a small group of leftist SHARP (Skinheads Against Racial Prejudice) Skins, many of those calling themselves "nationalist" or "patriotic" Skins do not necessarily subscribe to Nazi ideology. Some of the leading figures are, however, unabashed neo-Nazis and ideological racists.

The first tiny group, Boot Boys, started up in 1987. Their leader was (and still is) Ole Krogstad. He was a regional youth leader in the now-defunct and partly Nazi-inspired Nasjonalt Folkeparti (National People's Party). Together with other leading party activists, Krogstad was arrested in 1985 after a bomb attack on a Muslim mosque. The culprit in this attack was another young Skinhead member of Nasjonalt Folkeparti, but the police investigation brought other crimes to the surface. Krogstad was sentenced to 10 months imprisonment for a dynamite attack on an immigrant welfare office, painting Nazi slogans on a Jewish synagogue, and illegally possessing explosives and weapons. After serving his term, Krogstad became an activist in the now-defunct Nasjonal-Demokratisk Union.

Bodyguard Service

During the late eighties, Boot Boys linked up with the racist movement Folkebevegelsen Mot Innvandring (FMI, The People's Movement Against Immigration), and later its split-off Norge Mot Innvandring (NMI, Norway Against Immigration). The Boot Boys turned up as bodyguards at many of FMI's and NMI's rallies and meetings. These meetings regularly ended up in clashes with the police and/or the Skins' leftist SHARP opponents.

Partly on account of the small number of Norwegian "nationalist" Skins, they have had to cooperate with other (non-Skinhead) groups and individuals both in Norway and abroad. The Skinhead and Nazi movements in Sweden have always been admired by their Norwegian "smaller brothers." In 1991, some Norwegians were allowed to join the Swedish Nazi terrorist network Vitt Ariskt Motstånd (VAM, White Aryan Resistance). VAM is modeled after the American terrorist group The Order and its fictional version in "The Turner Diaries," a novel by the American neo-Nazi William Pierce. A Norwegian branch of VAM was set up during 1991 (HAM, Hvit Arisk Motstand), but it was soon exposed and deeply discredited (especially in relation to international Nazi circles) when one of its members turned out to be an anti-fascist mole. He went public and told the media and the police about plans to bomb a leftist youth club in Oslo and to set fire to the cottage belonging to the President of the Norwegian parliament, who is Jewish. After this blunder, the Norwegian "Aryan warriors" had to keep their heads low for a while.

New Groups

During 1992 and '93, a couple of new Skinhead-inspired groups surfaced. The first was Birkebeinerne (a name derived from an old Viking saga). The leading members of this group were identical with leaders of the Norwegian branch of the Swedish VAM (HAM), but they were also reinforced with some activists from NMI and the crumbling FMI. Unlike HAM, Birkebeinerne try to present themselves as non-Nazi nationalists. ("Selling" Nazism and patriotism in the same package is highly problematic in Norway, due to memories of the Norwegian Nazis' collaboration with German occupiers during the Second World War, which gave rise to the label "quislings," after the name of their leader.)

Another new local group is called Ariske Brødre (Aryan Brothers). Some members from Ariske Brødre have secretly cooperated with leading members of Fedrelandspartiet (The Fatherland Party). This party is the biggest anti-immigration party in Norway, having received around 12,000 votes in the 1993 election to the Norwegian parliament (0.6% of the total). A third group, with ambitions to serve as a kind of umbrella organization, is Norsk Ungdom/Ung Front (Norwegian Youth/Young Front). Skinheads comprise part of the membership of another recently formed group, Viking.

During spring 1993, members of the different Skinhead groups worked together in the planning of attacks on anti-fascist meetings. The attacks failed completely, as the police knew their plans in advance. Neither could these groups prevent the anti-fascist demonstrators from breaking up most rallies and meetings held by the racist Fedrelandspartiet in the Norwegian election campaign.

First Band

Late in the summer of 1994, the first Skinhead band, The Rinnan Band, surfaced in Norway. Henry Rinnan, after whom the band was named, was Nazi-occupied Norway's most hated and feared torturer. After threats of lawsuits from Rinnan's relatives, the band changed its name to H-band or the Hirdmen. That name, too, has an association with Nazism: although the old Norwegian Viking kings' bodyguards were called Hirdmen, the name was also used by the armed and uniformed followers of the Norwegian traitor Quisling during the Nazi occupation.

Dozens of Skinhead members of Viking, Ariske Brødre and Boot Boys were among over 75 extremists detained in Oslo in February 1995 after they attacked left-wing protestors with slingshots and other crude weapons. The incident took place at a building rented out by neo-Nazis and other extremist groups under the guise that it was a "cultural center." The police confiscated weapons as well as Nazi propaganda and paraphernalia from the building.

Since their arrival on the scene, Norwegian Skinheads have generally been looked upon as outcasts and madmen with their shaven heads and admiration of Adolf Hitler. Perhaps because of their modest numbers, the Skins and

other right-wing extremists have recently tried to recruit school children as young as 12 into their ranks, although these efforts so far have been unsuccessful. After seven years of activity, they number no more than 100 to 150 (but slowly growing), and their names and faces are well known.

However, to other Nazi groups and "respectable" anti-immigrant parties and organizations, the Skinheads are important as foot soldiers. Over the last couple of years they have helped more sophisticated Nazi groups to gather information about leading anti-fascists, politicians and journalists. A Norwegian harassment (and possibly death) list has been compiled by a secretive group called Anti-antifa (anti-anti-fascists). A leading member of Anti-antifa is a right-wing extremist who has been convicted of bombings and arms theft. He spent a short time in the French Foreign Legion, and his name has been linked to the Boot Boys. Together with other militarily experienced persons he is now trying to discipline both Skinheads and ordinary youth who have been dragged into the web of the Nazis. Their plan has two focuses: to establish a reign of terror in the streets (by the use of Skinheads) and by selective terror to silence their main political opponents.

POLAND

The Skinhead movement has found adherents in Poland where their violence has become deadly and their political extremism has escalated since the fall of Communism. The Polish Skinheads' anger and energy have been given direction by far-right nationalist forces.

Violent behavior is a hallmark of the Polish Skinheads. They seek out victims at mass gatherings, such as soccer matches and rock concerts. Smaller groups also single out individuals for assault. The Skinheads tend to avoid provoking the police, but have fought them on occasion when the police have tried to quell their disturbances. After an initial perception of spotty law enforcement, the police response to the Skinhead problem is regarded as having improved, particularly since the killing of a German truck driver in October 1992.

Hard-core racist Skinheads in Poland total approximately 2,000, along with twice that number of supporters and hangers-on. Skinhead activity has been observed in Warsaw, Krakow (especially the steel-producing suburb of Nowa Huta), Lodz, Katowice, Wroclaw (Breslau), Gdansk, Gdynia, Poznan, Sopot, Szczecin, Pulawy, Czestochowa and Legnica.

First Appearance

Skinheads first appeared on the Polish scene in the mid-1980's. In the period just before the collapse of the Communist regime, they engaged government forces in street battles. But soon afterward, a sizable number took a turn to the far right. In May 1990, Skins served as bodyguards at the First Congress of the Polish Right, where they beat up left-wing demonstrators protesting in front of the hall. The Skins were members of a nationalist group called Polish National Renewal (Narodowe Odrodzenie Polski). Skinheads again provided security at a convention of several nationalist parties in December 1992.

In 1993, National Radical Offensive (Ofensywa Narodowo Radykalna) was formed in Krakow by approximately 50 Skinheads, intending to harass leftists and to coordinate Skinhead groups. It has participated in a number of right-wing demonstrations.

Anti-Semitic and xenophobic rhetoric in the bitter and divisive presidential election of 1990 and the subsequent parliamentary elections further fueled the politicization of Polish Skinheads. Far-right political groups (most of them marginal) that have influenced them include the National Front of Poland (Narodowy Front Polski), the recently formed and similarly named Polish National Front (Polski Front Narodowy), several separate outfits that use the name National Party (Stronnictwo Narodowe), and, most notably, the Polish National Community/Polish National Party (Polska Wspolnota Narodowa/Polskie Stronnictwo Narodowe), led by Boleslaw Tejkowski. The PWN/PSN, which has enrolled Skinheads as party members, preaches that the Poles "are being ruled by Jewish nationalists" whom it maligns as former "Communist torturers" turned "capitalist exploiters." The "USA, Germany and Israel are taking over our national riches," says the party.

While older party members print and peddle leaflets and publications, it is the Skinheads who have heeded Tejkowski's appeals to demonstrate in the streets. The PWN/PSN maintains contacts with extremists in other countries, including Jean-Marie Le Pen's Front National in France, the Russian group Pamyat, and the Ukrainian Pan-Slavic Movement. Tejkowski also boasts of contacts with the North Korean and Iraqi embassies in Warsaw. During court proceedings against Tejkowski in February 1992, Skinheads demonstrated inside and outside the courthouse in Warsaw, and beat two journalists. Tejkowski was being tried for inciting Skinheads to attack Jews and others, but he went into hiding to avoid court-ordered psychiatric tests. In October 1994, Tejkowski was given a one-year suspended sentence, but was told that he would spend that time in jail if he resumed his activities within two years of the ruling. He declared that he would carry on in the same fashion despite the court's decision, reportedly vowing to "continue criticizing the authorities until they are overthrown."

"Poland for the Poles"

The targets of Skinhead propaganda and violence are so-called aliens, be they foreigners, Jews or punk rockers. Anti-Semitic slogans are routinely shouted at their demonstrations. In April 1995, for example, some 80 young men, most of them Skinheads, chanted "Down with the Jews" and "Poland for the Poles" during a demonstration in a Warsaw square. Skins yelled anti-Jewish slogans during an April 1992 ceremony to observe the 51st anniversary of the formation by the Nazis of the Jewish ghetto in Czestochowa. The Skinheads, who came from Krakow, Lodz, Poznan and Wroclaw, erupted in a vocal barrage as the Israeli Ambassador to Poland unveiled a commemorative plaque to the victims. Police quickly quelled the disturbance without any arrests. Skinheads and their allies have attempted to disrupt other Holocaust commemorations since then. Skins also have demonstrated in front of the Israeli embassy in Warsaw, and have burned an Israeli flag in Szczecin.

Violence aimed at Jews has been physical as well as rhetorical. In July 1991, Skinheads attacked a female student at Warsaw University who "looked Jewish," cutting her face with a razor. She lost an eye. The Jewish Historical Institute in Warsaw was attacked by a gang of Skinheads in November 1990. When they were unable to force the doors, they stoned the building, breaking windows. A police spokesman in Wroclaw said Skinheads were believed responsible for the destruction of 40 tombstones in that city's Jewish cemetery in April 1992. On Rosh Hashana (the Jewish New Year) in 1991, the Warsaw synagogue was attacked by a group of young thugs, including Skinheads, resulting in injuries to two elderly worshippers. Since that incident, the police have maintained a permanent presence near the synagogue.

Jewish Pope

Skinheads and other extremists frequently use the term "Jew" as a label for any of their targets regardless of whether they are actually Jewish. Pope John Paul II, Lech Walesa, numerous government officials and large numbers of priests and bishops are "Jews," according to the publication of the PWN/PSN.

Germans are also a target of the Polish Skinheads, who hold that a reunified Germany, along with increased German investment, poses a threat to Poland. Polish Skins are active in Silesia, an area with a German minority that Poland acquired from Germany after World War II, and that German revanchists yearn to recover.

Mutual Hatred

Hatred of foreigners has propelled both German and Polish Skinheads to commit violence against citizens of each other's countries. German Skinheads attacked a busload of Polish tourists on October 3, 1992, following an open-air concert in Massen that attracted more than 1,500 Skinheads. Two days earlier, three German truck drivers were attacked by a gang of Polish Skinheads in Nowa Huta. One of the victims was killed. The police quickly identified and arrested several suspects, and there was vigorous local condemnation of the killing. In Opole, in February 1992, Polish Skins attacked a group of Germans and Poles in a cafe, and beat other Poles who tried to intervene.

Others who have been assaulted are Arabs, Gypsies, and black students at universities in Krakow and Wroclaw. One of the Skinheads arrested for the killing of the German truck driver was already under investigation for the beating of two Arab students. A week after the assaults on the German truck drivers, another gang of Skinheads attacked a shelter in Bytom that housed Romanian Gypsies. In a separate incident, an elderly Gypsy woman was beaten by Skinheads in a December 1992 attack on Gypsy houses in Chorzow. In addition, while no violence broke out, a rally by 100 Skinheads in Krakow during March 1992 featured demands to "stop the inflow of foreigners." They were prevented by the police from marching to the former Soviet consulate to stage an anti-Ukrainian demonstration. Recently, cases of Skinheads beating up blind youth have also been reported.

In February 1995, a black American basketball player, Thomas Eggleton, who plays for the local team in the town of Stargard, was attacked by a group of Skinheads who shouted insults and beat him.

Skinhead Style

The Skinheads in Poland have adopted the accoutrements of their counterparts in the West: Doc Martens boots, narrow jeans and thin suspenders. They frequently wear T-shirts inscribed "Skinhead Oi."

Polish Skinhead bands (some of which may no longer be active) have included BTH, Grunwald, Ramses and the Hooligans, Szczerbiec (Sword), White Power, Slav Power, Zyklon B, Fatherland, Poland, Sex Bomba, Zadruga, Honor, Sztorm 68 and Legion. The bands Konkwista 88 and Falanga 88, both from Wroclaw, describe themselves as National Socialist ("88" is neo-Nazi code for "Heil Hitler," H being the eighth letter of the alphabet). Followers of Konkwista 88 and Falanga 88 attacked a gathering organized by black students to celebrate the release of Nelson Mandela from prison in South Africa.

News about the music scene fills the pages of Skinhead publications. Some Polish skinzines are *Szczerbiec, Kolomir, Skinhead Polski, Czas Mlodych* and *Krzyzowiec.* A piece written for a British skinzine by Polish Skinheads indicated that they have been in contact with their counterparts elsewhere in Europe, especially the former Czechoslovakia.

There are other international connections. The Swedish neo-Nazi Skinhead gang Vitt Ariskt Motstånd (White Aryan Resistance), for instance, has established contacts in Szczecin in the region of Pomerania. Some German neo-Nazi Skinheads had hoped to form an alliance with their Polish counterparts against "aliens" from further to the south and the east, but they have been stymied by Polish extremists' antagonism toward Germany. Ironically, Polish Skins — particularly those from Krakow and Nowa Huta — reportedly purchase their Skinhead gear from West Berlin suppliers.

"Too Much Dancing"

Some Skins in Poland apparently see an overemphasis on music as a detriment to their cause. "Man does not dance, but acts. There is too much dancing, too little work and struggle," one activist is quoted as saying. His choice of words suggests a certain debt owed by the Skinheads and their ultra-nationalist confederates to the rules of the old Communist regime. A Skinhead leader in Katowice has been exposed as a former agent of the disbanded Communist secret police, fueling suspicions by some in Poland that there may be others like him.

The attitude of Polish Skinheads toward the Catholic Church appears ambivalent. Skins staged an anti-abortion protest in Warsaw shouting "Catholic Poland — Sieg Heil!" But in Przemysl, in southeastern Poland, Skinheads threatened to beat up "any Polish priest who will dare say Mass" at a controversial proposed memorial for German soldiers in World War II. The threats in this case probably owe more to anti-German hostility than antipathy toward the Church. The Pope has denounced the "incredible ferocity" of neo-Nazi Skinheads and other hate groups as "cruel and dangerous," and has urged people to reject them.

PORTUGAL

Sporadic episodes of Skinhead violence have occurred in Portugal in the last several years. The U.S. Department of State, in its *Country Reports on Human Rights for 1993,* cited Portuguese press accounts of "a number of racially motivated incidents in 1993 that were apparently perpetrated by small, loosely knit 'skinhead' groups." The targets of Skinhead assaults have tended to be immigrants, both legal and illegal, from Portugal's former African colonies. A rampage by 50 Skinheads in Lisbon on June 11, 1995, left a Cape Verdean immigrant dead and 12 people of African origin injured. Nine Skins have been detained.

In October 1989, Jose Carvalho, a leftist activist, was killed in Lisbon by Skinheads who were demonstrating at the headquarters of the Socialist Revolutionary Party. Three other party members were injured in the attack.

Skinhead violence reportedly impelled the Portuguese government in 1990 to establish a committee to monitor the treatment of minority groups.

Several Skinhead gangs have displayed neo-Nazi symbols at matches of Benfica, a leading soccer team from Lisbon.

Two Lisbon-based publications, *As Runas* and *Final Solution,* have been advertised in foreign Skinhead and neo-Nazi publications.

A Portuguese Skinhead band, Guarda de Ferro (Iron Guard), has recorded on the French label Rebelles Européens. Its songs include such titles as "Skinheads," "Botas" (boots), and "Portugal aos Portugueses" (Portugal for the Portuguese).

SLOVAKIA

Numbering a few hundred, the Slovak Skinheads have attacked Gypsies (Roma), ethnic Hungarians, Jews, guest workers and those whose political views they abhor. Physical attacks attributed to Skinheads have taken place in Bratislava, Trnava, Košice, Prešov, and Skalica.

In the wake of the collapse of communism and the breakup of Czechoslovakia, segments of the Slovak population have sought scapegoats for their current difficult times. There has been some public support for Skinhead attacks against foreigners and Gypsies, groups commonly blamed for many of the country's problems. The police themselves have been accused of failing to respond adequately to Skinhead attacks against members of the substantial Roma community.

Skinheads have vandalized Jewish cemeteries and synagogues, and they have held occasional public rallies replete with the chanting of anti-Semitic slogans. Further, Skins have attacked participants at rallies and concerts against fascism.

As elsewhere, Slovakia's Skinheads are divided into two groups: (1) hard-core racists who follow the Skinhead lifestyle, and (2) sympathizers (particularly football hooligans) who follow Skinhead fashions, share some of the Skins' views and have a similar taste for violence.

There is at least one Slovak Skinhead band: Kratky Proces (Short Process), whose first LP was highly praised by the British skinzine *Last Chance*.

SLOVENIA

Slovenian Skinheads have stated that they first appeared in public in 1984, when the country was still part of Yugoslavia. A small group of them began to hang around the punk scene, frequenting music clubs in the capital city, Ljubljana. As their number grew, the Skinheads took to congregating on Friday nights in pubs in Ljubljana. Most Skins were from southern Slovenia, but some traveled from other parts of the country to attend the gatherings. The hangouts would change when their trouble-making caused them to be banned from particular pubs. They also developed a reputation for starting fights at concerts around the city.

One incident in 1989 brought the Slovenian Skinheads much attention. Fighting broke out at a concert billed as "New Rock," attended by some 2,500 young people, most of them punk rockers, hippies, and heavy metal fans, but also some 25 Skinheads. A heavy metal fan was killed, and the police arrested approximately 15 Skinheads. Slovenian Skins claim that the publicity about this incident resulted in a substantial increase in membership.

Today, the Skinhead scene remains centered primarily in the capital. Skins belong to a Slovenian National Socialist movement known as Mladi Domobran (Young Militia Men or Home Guard), which borrows its name from World War II-era Slovenian Nazis. They distribute a propaganda organ called *Rudi*, which promotes their ultranationalist and extremist views.

The xenophobic Slovenian National Party (SNS), led by Zmago Jelincic, reportedly has sought to attract Skinheads and other right-wing young people to its ranks. The SNS, using the slogan "Slovenia for the Slovenes," won 9.9 percent of the vote in elections for the national State Assembly in December 1992, entitling it to 12 of the Assembly's 90 seats. Recent opinion polls, however, indicate the party's support has slipped considerably.

SOUTH AFRICA

Schooled as they are in Nazi racial doctrine, and stirred by the sermons of violence resounding in their own music, it was not unexpected that Skinheads would exercise their disaffection in the new society in South Africa.

There are known to be Skins active in South Africa, although estimates of their number are difficult to come by. Most are active in the Johannesburg area. In one suburb, Yeoville, there are reported to be 20 Skinheads, mostly English-speaking, who have at times displayed a Nazi flag, along with the banner of the paramilitary neo-Nazi Afrikaner Resistance Movement (AWB). Late in 1992, there were several incidents in Yeoville in which blacks were beaten by Skinheads; in one such attack an apartment was firebombed.

Skins have more recently been observed with their boots and heavily tattooed bodies at rallies of the AWB, headed by the terrorist Eugene Terreblanche. One Skinhead has reported that many Skins hold positions of rank in the AWB.

SPAIN

One Spanish Skinhead identifies the enemy: "I just attack scum, such as punks, anarchists, drug addicts.... We must kick them out of Europe. They stink. We don't want them. Let's get them."

This Skinhead, named Oscar, was interviewed by the Spanish journal *El Pais* in December 1993. He continued: "Dark-skinned people repel me. I love Spain, and I don't like people who don't belong to the white race to come here.... The white race is the one that must rule. We whites know that we are superior.... Spain needs a dictatorship."

Oscar, 19 years old, had just returned to Madrid from a bash in another city. On the train he and other Skins had beaten and kicked a man for being black.

"Decidedly Dangerous"

Skinheads were first seen in Spain in 1984 among the Ultra Sur fans of the Real Madrid Soccer Club. According to studies made by Spain's new Police Citizen Relations Operative Office, there were some 2,000 Skinheads in the country in late 1993 — half of them in Barcelona, one third in Madrid, the rest mainly in Valencia. (These are predominantly industrial cities with high population densities and large numbers of immigrants.) Of the 2,000 Skinheads, some 600 were radical right-wing extremists considered "decidedly dangerous." The rest appeared to assume the Skinhead "look" without the radical ideology.

The radical Skins are of the middle and lower classes and range in age from 15 to 22. (At 23, many seem to "retire" from the active bully life.) The *El Pais* interviewer suggested a profile of Spain's Nazi Skinheads: fairly obedient children, but poor students, who behave normally until the weekend, when they go out in packs of eight or 10 to attack their foes — blacks, immigrants, addicts. "The night, the big city, the nicknames — protect their anonymity."

Spanish Skinheads have cooperative links with other organized extremists groups. Among these groups are Juntas Españolas (Spanish Councils), a far-right nationalist party that opposes immigration, and Las Bases Autónomas, a network of far-right groups that has claimed responsibility for the same kind of street thuggery typical of Skinheads.

A notorious case was the November 1992 murder of a female Dominican immigrant by a Skinhead member of the police force (known as the Civil Guard). He and his three teenage accomplices (who had ties to Las Bases Autónomas) all received heavy sentences. In addition to attacking immigrants, Spanish Skins have repeatedly targeted homosexuals for beatings and — in at least one case — murder.

Go Team!

Skinheads continue to plague Spanish soccer. Although members of the aforementioned Ultra Sur gang have been denied admission to a number of stadiums, Skinheads are still seen brandishing Nazi symbols at matches of the major clubs in Madrid and Barcelona.

The proliferation of violent incidents (more than 40 per year in Madrid alone) spurred the creation in 1993 of the 30-member Special Police Group designed to centralize information and coordinate activity against organized youth violence. All information on Skin groups and individuals, until then uncoordinated, has been centralized, along with the arrest and booking process.

One initial Skinhead reaction to this development was to "camouflage" themselves in normal appearance, casting away the Doc Martens boots and letting their hair grow. Late in 1993, however, it seemed to be Skinhead business as usual, when the British skinzine, *Last Chance,* (1) announced the appearance of *Crew Zine,* a new Skinhead publication emanating from Madrid; (2) carried an advertisement for a second publication, *Skinhead del Sur de Europa,* from Barcelona; (3) announced that there were several Skinhead shops in Spain ("the best" being the Coyote Shop in Valencia); and (4) reviewed new recordings by Spain's "Division 250" Skin band.

"Heil! We are Nazis!"

Music has been an important element of Skinhead life in Spain for at least a decade. In the 1980's the Skin band Gabinete Caligari opened its performances with a cry of "Heil! We are Nazis!" Another, Los Ilegales, had a song titled "Heil Hitler."

On the 14th of March 1992, the Skin band Division 250 organized an international festival in Valencia, hosting invited guests from England, France, Italy, Belgium and Portugal — to hear the popular British bands Violent Storm, No Remorse, and Battle Zone, along with Division 250. (Violent Storm could not appear; only one of its members survived an auto crash on the way to Heathrow Airport for their flight to Spain.) No Remorse thrilled the international assemblage with a hit song lamenting that

> ... in 1933 the fight for race was won,
> But sadly those days of hope are gone ...
> We are all fighting tougher odds
> We look for guidance from the white man's gods.

SWEDEN

In the past 10 years, Swedish Skinheads have become an important part of the broader Swedish racist movement. They have served as bodyguards and security forces for various neo-Nazi organizations, and in the name of Aryan supremacy, Skinheads have beaten, robbed and even killed perceived enemies.

Experts in Sweden currently put the number of skinheads at well over 1,000, of whom some 100 to 200 are considered "especially dangerous." The overall figure includes a large number of so-called "Babyskins," a term coined by police in 1994 to refer to the rising number of very young Skinheads recruited from schools in several communities.

The major populations centers — Stockholm, Gothenburg, and Malmö — contain the largest concentrations of Skins. Smaller numbers are active in Norrköping, Linköping, Karlstad, Södertälje, Växjö, Säffle and Uddevalla.

Storm

Swedish Skinheads have been heavily influenced by *Storm,* a neo-Nazi magazine that was launched in 1990 as the successor to an earlier racist publication, *Vit Rebell* (White Rebel).* *Storm* mixes classic Nazi anti-Semitism with other anti-Jewish conspiracy theories. The magazine singles out the Jews as the main cause of Sweden's political and economical difficulties. The battle against immigration has failed, according to *Storm,* on account of Jewish domination of the media, the banks and the government. Hence, says the magazine, the battle against Jewry is paramount, and must be waged through armed struggle. No new issues of *Storm* have been published since fall 1994.

With *Storm* apparently publishing intermittently, three new magazines have begun to fill the void: *Nordland; Blod och Ära* (Blood and Honor), last published in October 1994; and *Gryning* (Dawn), published by and for Skinheads in prison.

Storm has become the single most important expression of Skinhead "philosophy" in Sweden. The magazine offers broad political direction to Swedish Skinheads — and has given rise to the "Storm Network," an informal structure of cooperation and political unity among several neo-Nazi Skinhead organizations. The most important groups in the Network are:

Vitt Ariskt Motstånd (VAM, White Aryan Resistance), formed in 1991 as "a vehicle for racial war" along the lines of the American far-right terrorist group, The Order. At its peak, VAM consisted of at least 150 hard-core activists and perhaps twice as many supporters. Its structure, like that of most Skinhead gangs, is loose and informal; there are no membership cards, elected officials or formal gatherings. VAM activists have been convicted of a number of violent crimes, including several armed robberies and gun thefts. In the recent year, VAM has gone through a political reorientation, attempting to transform itself from an underground militant group to a semi-legal street organization.

Riksfronten (The Reich Front), now led by Torulf Magnusson. The group has emerged as the political face of Skinhead militancy. It is believed to have at least a few hundred members.

The Church of the Creator (COTC), led by "Reverend" Tommy Rydén and Skinhead David Twaland (a.k.a. Emilsson). This is the Swedish branch of the now-inactive American neo-Nazi mother church. Although the Swedish

---

* *Vit Rebell* was founded in 1988 with the help of the British Skinhead leader Ian Stuart. It folded after its publishers were charged (they were later convicted) with violating Sweden's anti-racist laws.

group has only a handful of members, it is believed to have a large influence on the Storm Network.

While the Storm Network was formed outside the control of the traditional extreme right parties in Sweden, the Skinhead movement is linked with the two principal racist parties: the anti-immigrant Sweden Democrats, and the traditionally Hitlerite Nordic Reich Party (NRP), which has a few hundred supporters.

Armed Struggle

Swedish Skinheads have committed a great many crimes over the past four years, more than can be listed here. Among the most notorious ones have been the following:

In April 1991, four masked men raided a police station in a Stockholm suburb and made off with 40 handguns. Two of the culprits, both VAM activists, were subsequently arrested and are presently serving jail time.

In May 1991, seven Skinheads were arrested during an attempted burglary at a military arms depot in northern Sweden. One of the group, John-Christopher Rangne, is believed to be a leading member of VAM.

Two Skinheads were captured following an armed bank robbery in 1991. One was convicted and sentenced to six years in prison; the other was released for lack of evidence.

In January 1992, former Reich Front leader Leif Larsson was convicted of assault, and sentenced to a year in prison.

Also in January 1992, three Skinheads were arrested for possession of army materiel stolen from a military arms depot. One of those arrested was David Twaland, deputy leader of the Church of the Creator.

In May 1992, in Uppsala, four Skinheads were arrested and subsequently convicted of illegal possession of weapons in connection with a plot to rob a bank.

In August 1992, six Skinheads were arrested in a VAM safehouse containing arms, ammunition and other stolen military hardware. Two were subsequently convicted, but the charges against the remaining four were dropped.

In November 1992, VAM activist Stefan Lund was captured and sentenced to five years in prison for his role in an armed bank robbery. His partners-in-crime are still missing, as are the 1.5 million Kronor in stolen loot.

Skinhead crimes against Jews have, until now, consisted mainly of desecrations of graves and threats against individuals.

International Ties

The Swedish Skinhead movement has forged extensive links with hate movements in other countries, especially Britain and the United States. Skinheads first appeared in the streets of Sweden in the mid to late 1970's, when they were viewed as simply another fringe youth cult — like the punks or rockers — with their own style of dress and brand of music. However, they shortly developed a distinctly fascist outlook. Swedish Nazi groups had influenced them somewhat, but from England came the very potent impact of a full-blown Skinhead movement replete with racial ideology and music. Britain's leading Skinhead band, Skrewdriver, twice played in Sweden, in 1987 and 1989. During the first visit, Skrewdriver's leader, Ian Stuart, met with the Swedish Skins and made arrangements to help them publish a newspaper, the afore-mentioned *Vit Rebell*. During the same period, an English Skinhead, Tommy Edwards, became active in the leadership of the Swedish movement and served as liaison with its British comrades.

There have also been links to the American hate movement — for example, the formation in Sweden of a unit of the Church of the Creator. The Swedish branch, like the American, actively sought Skinheads recruits, with some measure of success.

The pages of *Storm* magazine also reflect considerable contact with American neo-Nazis, particularly the imprisoned members of The Order, the terrorist organization that murdered Denver talk radio host Alan Berg in 1984, and committed other serious crimes. From their prison cells, Order members David Lane, Frank Silva, Bruce Carroll Pierce, and Gary Yarbrough have been in correspondence with the publishers of *Storm*. They are, in effect, serving as advisors to the Swedish Skinhead movement, thereby intensifying its anti-Semitism and proclivity to terrorism.

Much American printed hate material circulates among the Swedish Skinheads. "The Turner Diaries," a novel by William Pierce, leader of the National Alliance, a West Virginia-based Nazi group, is a particular favorite. The book, which served as the bible of The Order, offers a blueprint on how to conduct a violent Aryan revolution. Printed materials also come from the American Nazi Gary Lauck, who publishes the organ *Sveriges Nationella Förbund* (Swedish National League) for the neo-Nazi organization of the same name. The League's Malmö unit, headed by 35-year-old Lars-Göran Hedengard, is affiliated with Lauck's Nebraska-based NSDAP-AO (National Socialist German Workers Party-Overseas Organization).

Lauck linked up with Hedengard during a trip to Sweden in 1990. The name of the Skinhead group White Aryan Resistance (Vitt Ariskt Motstånd, VAM) is identical with that of the American Nazi organization, WAR, headed by Tom Metzger, which was the first to use it. However, VAM's attitudes more closely resemble those of The Order and Aryan Nations.

The Music Scene

Sweden's Skinheads are also linked to their counterparts abroad through their bands. Dirlewanger, a leading Swedish Skinhead band, played at an Aryan fest in southern California in September 1992. The band also has close ties to the German Skinhead scene. (Dirlewanger was the name of a German SS officer, Oskar Dirlewanger, who commanded an *Einsatzkommando* unit on the eastern front in World War II.) The traffic runs both ways, with foreign Skinhead bands — among them the British bands No Remorse and Bully Boys — appearing in Sweden as well.

There have been several other bands active in the Swedish Skinhead musical scene, including Vit Aggression (White Agression), Division S, Agent Bulldog, Midgard Soner, Svastika and Ultima Thule (which has successfully entered the mainstream).

On February 4, 1995, several hundred Skinheads turned out for a white power concert in Stockholm that featured Division S, Midgard Soner and Svastika. According to the California-based zine *Blood and Honor,* the American band Bound For Glory also made an appearance.

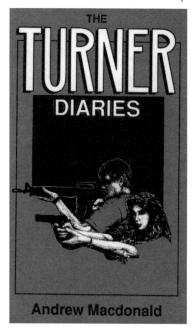

Since about 1993, Skinhead music — compact discs as well as videos — has become a principal source of income for individual Skinheads and Skinhead political organizations. A number of Nazi mail order outlets have sprung up, providing substantial revenue. Few, if any, major record shops in Sweden sell Skinhead recordings, but during 1994, several Skinhead-owned shops opened in Stockholm and Gothenburg.

The Icehouse

A popular Skinhead hangout in Stockholm is Fryshuset (the Icehouse), a youth club partly funded by the local authorities in the (questionable) belief that it would "keep them off the streets." The Skins formerly had their own (partly state-subsidized) headquarters, located alongside Fryshuset. Piles of copies of the British Skinhead magazine *Blood and Honour* and the American Nazi publications *Racial Loyalty* and "The Turner Diaries" were seen in the headquarters.

Finally, as stated earlier, Swedish Skinheads are part of the broader Swedish hate movement, although their relationship is sometimes strained. That was the case in 1988, when the far-right Sweden Democrats (SD) party was launched. The party was formed by persons long steeped in racism, who decided to clean up their public image in the hope that it would broaden their appeal, in the style of the French Front National. Since Skinheads hardly fit the desired new image, they were disavowed.

The SD strategy paid off. The party's membership grew; it got 4,900 votes in the 1991 parliamentary elections and 14,000 votes in 1994 (much higher numbers than usual for an ultra-right party in Sweden). The SD now has five seats in local assemblies. Nevertheless, there has been growing evidence that despite its protestations to the contrary, the SD's back-door links with the Skinheads were never actually broken, or, if broken, have been restored.

SWITZERLAND

Skinheads and other neo-Nazi extremists in Switzerland number about 250, mainly in the northeastern part of the country. They have, in addition, perhaps a few hundred sympathizers.

A Skinhead gang known as the Schweizer (Swiss) Hammer Skins has operated in the towns of Littau, just west of Luzern, and Schwyz, about 25 kilometers to the east. Their choice of the moniker "Hammer Skins" suggests a likely influence from similarly named gangs in the United States. Another Skinhead gang, Neo-Faschistischen Front (Neo-fascist Front), recently appeared. Based in Bern, the group claims members in Basel and Zurich as well as in Germany.

Neo-Nazis and other far-rightists reportedly have been responsible for a number of anti-foreigner and anti-Jewish incidents in Switzerland. Several attacks on refugees occurred in 1993, including three arson attempts against asylum residences. The number of attacks was down, however, from the two previous years. Arson was suspected in fires that killed five asylum seekers in 1992, but no arrests were made. Spray-painted graffiti on refugee hostels reportedly has included Nazi slogans.

The number of anti-Semitic incidents in Switzerland reportedly rose markedly following the Skinhead-led anti-foreigner riots in Rostock, Germany, in the autumn of 1992. In January 1993, two Skinheads made offensive remarks to security guards at a Zurich synagogue at which services were taking place.

Sturmtruppen
A Skinhead band from Reinach, southwest of Zurich, has given voice to the same racist, anti-foreigner themes as have their comrades elsewhere. Known as Sturmtruppen (Stormtroopers), the group has recorded an album ("It Is Time") for the German label Rock-O-Rama Records. Their song "Kanikistan Is Burning" envisions thousands of Skins pushing eastward to reduce "Kanikistan" — a fictitious land whose name derives from a derogatory

term for foreigners, especially Turks — to rubble and ash.

In an interview in a German skinzine called *Querschläger*, two members of Sturmtruppen described themselves as "nationalists" (but denied they are Nazis), and claimed membership in the Nationalistischen Jugend Schweiz (Nationalist Youth of Switzerland). The band's "nationalism" finds expression in their song "Switzerland," whose lyrics glorify "pure race, pure blood," as well as the Swiss flag, Swiss cross, Swiss women and Swiss beer. The lyrics also declare solidarity with "Comrades of European countries" who are "pure Aryan."

At least one skinzine, called *Totenkopf* (after the Death's Head emblem employed by Hitler's SS), has been produced in Switzerland. It has been distributed from mailing addresses in Luzern, and, later, the town of Horw, just to the south. According to the British anti-fascist magazine *Searchlight*, the pages of *Totenkopf* have featured interviews with European, American and Brazilian Skinhead bands, advertisements for right-wing extremist groups, and racist propaganda.

UNITED KINGDOM

The Skinhead phenomenon had its birth in the United Kingdom, arising as a youth cult in the early 1970's, and Britain is still regarded as the fountainhead of the movement worldwide. It was there that the Skinhead aspect and regalia developed — shaved heads, boots, tattoos — designed to symbolize tough, angry, rebellious working-class youth. (The steel-toed Doc Martens boots, *de rigueur* for Skins everywhere, are manufactured in Britain.) Along with the style went fixed attitudes: an extreme nationalism, a brash male chauvinism, a glorification of brute violence. Before long, a large number of British Skinheads were also displaying hostility towards non-whites, Jews, foreigners and homosexuals. Filling out the format was "oi" music ("oi" is a Cockney greeting), which — for the racist Skins — meant the threatening sound of "white power."

Present estimates of the number of British Skinheads vary from some 1,500 to as many as 2,000. These figures represent a slight decline over the past year or two.

Blood and Honour

The main Skinhead "organization" is Blood and Honour, a loose sort of structure founded in 1987 by Ian Stuart Donaldson— professionally (and hereinafter) "Ian Stuart" — a Skinhead musician who was killed in an automobile crash in Derbyshire late in 1993. Stuart's band, Skrewdriver, has been for years the most popular Skinhead group in Britain and throughout the world. Under the name The Klansmen, the band has made records for the United States market — one of their songs was titled "Fetch the Rope." Stuart always preferred being called a Nazi rather than a "neo-Nazi." He once told the London *Evening Standard*: "I admire everything Hitler did, apart from one thing — losing."

Stuart's legacy, Blood and Honour (its name is the translation of an SS slogan) is a frenzied amalgam of racist lore and music. Organically it has been described as not so much a political organization as "a neo-Nazi street movement." Influential among Skinheads throughout Europe and the United States, Blood and Honour acts as an umbrella organization for 30 or more Skin rock groups, publishes a magazine (also called *Blood and Honour*)* and runs a mail order service for "white pride" paraphernalia, which is said to have thousands of accounts.

The Skinhead bands affiliated with the Blood and Honour movement have their own security guards. Not known for their restraint, these guards often battle perceived enemies at clubs where the bands perform and on the street.

Since Stuart's death, Blood and Honour has reportedly fallen under the influence of Combat 18 (18 is code for Adolf Hitler's initials), a violent neo-Nazi group that counts Skinheads and football hooligans among its followers.

"You don't become a member of Blood and Honour," a BBC report stated. "You support it by buying the records, carrying the flag, wearing the T-shirts and the tattoos."

And sometimes by other means...

"Paki-bashing"

Assaults on Asians ("Paki-bashing") and homosexuals ("fag-bashing") have become standard forms of Skinhead brutality, as have desecrations of synagogues and Jewish cemeteries. A march through South East London protesting racial violence recently was disrupted by Skinheads who pelted the marchers with bricks and bottles. The Skins then turned on the police whom they forced to retreat by attacking them with stones and crash barriers.

On the night of September 11, 1993, 30 neo-Nazi Skinheads marched through Brick Lane in the heart of a predominantly Asian neighborhood, breaking shop windows and menacing residents. "We're being deprived of what's ours," a young Skinhead was quoted in the newspapers a few nights later, "but we're fighting back now!"

Many Skins have served time. Kev Turner, leader of the popular Skin band Skullhead, for example, can boast a 20-month sentence for assault. Another Skullhead regular, Neil Carter, was jailed for nine months for his part in an attack on a nightclub owner.

---

* Similarly named publications have also appeared in California and Sweden.

Football Hooligans

Skinheads are fanatical supporters of certain English soccer (football) teams. Along with the more numerous football hooligans — many of whom share their neo-Nazi views — Skinheads are among the ringleaders of the racism and violence that plague English soccer. Skinheads are frequently seen at matches making Nazi salutes and taunting black players with vicious racist barbs. Violence, however, is their specialty. Joined by non-Skinhead members of Combat 18 and unaffiliated hooligans, Skins attack other fans (both rivals and fellow supporters) and run riot through stadiums, pubs and train stations. While the mayhem is often spontaneous, there is increasing evidence that soccer-related violence is sometimes planned in advance and orchestrated by a few dozen individuals, many of whom have a neo-Nazi agenda.

Neo-fascist Connections

A number of hard-core Skinheads have been active in several neo-fascist groups that have long tried to control the Skinhead scene. Most prominent among these are the racist and anti-Semitic British National Party (BNP), and the aforementioned Combat 18. The BNP participates in elections and enjoys small pockets of support in areas of London, Yorkshire and Lancashire. Combat 18, with a core of between 100 and 150 members, is committed to violence and harassment rather than political gains. While Skinheads formerly identified with the BNP — and reportedly assisted in some of its initial modest electoral success — they have increasingly switched their allegiance to Combat 18 in recent years.

Rock 'n' Roll

The message of the Skinheads booms from their music. It is violent, racist, paranoid, and "Nordic." All of the bands seem to catch the spirit of one called British Standard when it sings:

> The Iron Guard of Europe
> Has risen from the grave
> They march along as one now
> A New Order they must save.

Skrewdriver's "White Rider" brays:

> You feel love for your people
> Disdain for the fools
> The enemies led by the Zionist tools....

Last Chance, a now-defunct British skinzine, recently reviewed the first Skrewdriver album to be recorded after Ian Stuart's fatal car crash late in 1993:

Tunes such as "Hail Victory," "Vampire," and "White Noise," would, it said, "bring a tear to many eyes."

Another auto accident — this one in March 1992 — killed three of the four members of the group Violent Storm, whose home was Cardiff, Wales. They were on their way to Heathrow Airport for a flight to Spain, where they were scheduled to perform at a Skinhead concert that featured other British bands. The lone survivor, "Billy," later joined "Miffy," "Clarkey," and "Stinko" in a new band, Celtic Warrior, to "sing about the things we feel are important" — such as the "evils of Zionism" and the struggle for "our race."

The visions of the Skinhead mind are starkly reflected in some of the bands' names: Brutal Attack (whose album is pictured below), Battle Zone, Razor's Edge, No Remorse (this last referring specifically to the memory of the Holocaust). The recurrent theme of British Skinhead music is that only a race war, with the inner cities as battlegrounds, will bring about the reclamation of British soil. A popular song by Skrewdriver, "White Warriors," epitomizes this:

BRUTAL ATTACK

STRONGER THAN BEFORE

Fighting in the city,
It's a matter of life and death,
It's as easy as black and white,
You'll fight till your last breath...
When the battle is over,
And the victory is won,
The White man's lands are owned
By the White people,
The traitors will all be gone.

The steamy enthusiasm of Britain's Skinheads is kept at a high pitch by an abundance of zines published by a huge amateur underground network. The zines, such as *Blood and Honour, Boots and Braces, Truth at Last, British Oi!, Offensive Weapon* and *Aryan Warrior,* are mostly crude, slapdash photocopy productions comprising events calendars, ads, interviews, fan photos, letters, Skin gossip, etc., and abounding in Nazi and Odinist imagery. They also serve as effective links with their brethren on the Continent and across the globe.

Whether or not the reports of a slow decline in Skinhead numbers are accurate, it is generally agreed by those who monitor their activities that the Skinheads of Britain represent no mere passing fad — as the very longevity of the phenomenon shows. Having weathered 20 years of ebb and flow, it continues to poison young minds, perpetrate group violence and sing its vicious joy to the bewitched.

UNITED STATES

Neo-Nazi Skinheads first appeared on America's streets in the mid-eighties and have since shown substantial growth. From a membership of 1,000 to 1,500 in 12 states in early 1988, their ranks swelled to between 3,300 and 3,500 in 40 states by 1993. These numbers have held essentially steady since then.*

The growth in membership has been paralleled by an extraordinary record of violence. American Skins have graduated from the use of boots, bats and knives to using firearms. Indeed, the relative availability of guns in the United States has made American Skins among the most dangerous and violent in the world. Only the German Skinheads have consistently matched their American counterparts in the frequency and ferocity of their attacks.

This propensity for extreme acts of violence is reflected in the dramatic rise in the number of murders committed by Skinheads in the United States. From December 1987 to June 1990, there were a total of six such killings; in the three years that followed, no fewer than 22 more took place; since June 1993, an additional nine homicides have occurred for an overall total of at least 37.

Most of the Skinheads' murder victims have been members of minority groups: Hispanics, blacks, Asians, homosexuals and homeless persons. Some deaths have resulted from in-group violence, with Skinheads killing fellow gang members over, for instance, a pair of boots, a jacket, or some money. American Skinheads have also committed thousands of lesser crimes: beatings, stabbings, shootings, thefts, synagogue desecrations and other forms of mayhem and intimidation.

There is no single national Skinhead organization in the United States. Instead, loosely linked networks of Skinhead gangs operate in scattered communities. The gangs frequently change names and network affiliations. Individual members are often highly mobile, with little to tie them to a particular location. It is not uncommon for a group to leave a city and resume activity in another locale after feeling pressure from law enforcement and the community.

---

* In addition to the full-blown Skinheads there are at least an equal number of so-called "wanna-be's," youngsters who aspire to the status of regular Skinheads. The wanna-be's mimic the dress and style of Skinheads, listen to their "oi" music, and share many of their prejudices. They are usually young people living in areas where there are no organized Skinheads gangs; alternatively, they remain outside the ranks of actual Skins because they are fearful of the consequences of "coming out."

Broken Homes

Contrary to their claim to represent working-class youth, American Skinheads come from widely varying economic backgrounds. Their roots often lie not in economic decay but in domestic instability: a high proportion of American Skinheads come from broken homes or single-parent families. Their gangs — like other American youth gangs — often serve as surrogate families for their members. They frequently live in communal homes and apartments. Those who live with their families often do so under tense conditions; parents rarely approve of their Skinhead children's views or way of life.

This kind of domestic discord was tragically illustrated in February of this year when two Skinhead brothers were accused of bludgeoning and stabbing to death their mother, father and younger brother in their home near Allentown, Pennsylvania. Following the murders, the two fled to Michigan to meet up with other Skins whom they had met at a Skinhead music concert. They have since been brought back to Pennsylvania, where they await trial. The teenage brothers, both over six feet tall and weighing more than 200 pounds, were immersed in neo-Nazi Skinhead culture and had Nazi symbols and slogans tattooed on their bodies and foreheads. The boys' Nazi views were evidently at the center of an ongoing conflict with their parents, a religious couple who had struggled to turn the sons away from their hateful way of life, right up until the time of the murders.

Pack Mentality

The Skinhead Nazi ideology offers alienated youth self-esteem through the degradation of others. Their glorification of violence provides a sense of power; the pack mentality provides a sense of security.

American Skinheads pattern their dress on the original British model: combat boots or Doc Martens, thin suspenders and bomber jackets. Many are heavily tattooed with emblems of white supremacy and Nazism. While most still wear their hair closely cropped, some have taken to letting it grow in order to make themselves less conspicuous to law enforcement and the civilized public.

Some American Skinheads are known to use drugs (their anti-drug posturing notwithstanding), but virtually all are heavy beer drinkers. Typically, drinking binges precede hunts for purported "enemies."

Soon after their initial appearance in America, the Skinheads began to hook up with more organized racists and anti-Semites. In 1985, a small group of Skins from Chicago, dressed in full regalia, appeared at a gathering of hate group activists at the farm of a former Michigan Ku Klux Klan leader. Back in Chicago, under the name "Romantic Violence," they peddled tapes of the British Skinhead band Skrewdriver.

Marching with the Klan

Skinheads were soon marching in Klan demonstrations. At a January 1993 march in Pulaski, Tennessee (the birthplace of the KKK), about 100 Skinheads marched with Ku Kluxers, shouting anti-Jewish and white supremacist slogans.

As they outgrow the youthful Skinhead demeanor, some Skins actually join the KKK. Foremost among ex-Skinheads now in the Klan ranks is Shawn Slater. During the eighties, Slater was a well-known leader of the Denver Skins. In 1990, he began forging an alliance with the Klan. By 1992, Slater was leading a Klan rally in Denver. He and his followers subsequently switched affiliation from the Knights of the KKK to a more radical Klan faction.

The Skinheads have also linked up with such other old-line hate groups as the Aryan Nations, the Church of the Creator, and Tom Metzger's White Aryan Resistance (WAR). These older groups refer to the Skins as their "front-line warriors."

WAR has provided ideological and tactical direction to large numbers of Skinheads who have heeded Metzger's call for violence against minorities. This alliance reached its low when, on November 12, 1988, Mulugeta Seraw, a 27-year-old Ethiopian immigrant, was beaten to death by three members of the

Skinhead gang East Side White Pride in Portland, Oregon. Investigation into the murder revealed links between the gang and WAR. The Skinheads were convicted of the killing and are currently serving long sentences. In a subsequent civil lawsuit brought by the Anti-Defamation League and the Southern Poverty Law Center on behalf of Seraw's family, a jury determined that the Skinheads were incited to commit the crime by Metzger and his son, John. A $12.5 million judgment for Seraw's family was awarded on October 22, 1990.

Despite his legal setback, Metzger continues to influence Skinheads both at home and abroad from his base in southern California. Swedish and Australian Skinhead gangs have adopted the WAR name or acronym. Domestically, Metzger continues to proffer guidance and inspiration through his publication and telephone hotline, and he targets Skinhead buyers with his mail-order sales of racist "oi" music and videotapes of Skin music festivals.

Like Metzger's WAR, the Church of the Creator (COTC), a militant white supremacist and anti-Jewish group, has courted Skinheads since the 1980's. Skinhead members of the COTC have been responsible for serious episodes of violence in Wisconsin, California and Washington. More recently the "church" has splintered and become inactive in the U.S.

The Aryan Nations has for years hosted youth gatherings at its rural Idaho compound. These events, usually held in April to coincide with Hitler's birthday, have attracted numerous Skinheads. The April 1995 weekend featured performances by Skin bands Bound For Glory, Christian Identity Skins, and Odin's Law, a Canadian group.

Gary Lauck, of Lincoln, Nebraska, has made a 20-year career of furnishing Nazi propaganda to the world's extremists, Skinheads among them. For the last several years, Skinheads throughout Europe (especially Germany),

Latin America and the United States have been a target audience for Lauck's materials, which he produces in 12 languages. Lauck attempts to enlist Skinheads in his Nazi cause, asserting that they are "members of the great world-historical Aryan racial movement." One issue of *The New Order*, the organ of Lauck's NSDAP-AO (National Socialist German Workers Party-Overseas Organization), outlined his Action Program for Aryan Skinheads:

> Skinheads are realizing that they must primarily use their brains and apply their intelligence to outthink, outsmart, outplan, and outdo the racial enemy Jew System in the Race War.

Lauck was arrested in Denmark on March 20, 1995, pursuant to an international warrant issued by German authorities. If he is extradited to Germany, he faces charges of distributing illegal propaganda and Nazi symbols, incitement, encouraging racial hatred and belonging to a criminal group.

"God Forgive Me..."

American Skinheads have repeatedly acted out their racial warrior fantasies in acts of exceptional violence. In August 1990, in Houston, Texas, two 18-year-old Skinheads stomped a 15-year-old Vietnamese boy to death. One of the killers testified at his trial that the victim's last words were: "God forgive me for coming to this country. I'm so sorry." In a June 1991 drive-by shotgun slaying in Arlington, Texas, three 16-year-old members of the Confederate Hammerskins killed a black man while he sat on the back of a truck with two white friends.

Skinheads belonging to the Aryan National Front (ANF) were responsible for two separate killings of homeless black men in Birmingham, Alabama. One was beaten to death under a downtown viaduct before dawn on Christmas Eve 1991. He had been clubbed with a baseball bat and kicked repeatedly with heavy boots. One of the Skinhead perpetrators was convicted by a jury; another pled guilty to the murder. The second Birmingham killing occurred on April 18, 1992, the night after about 75 Skinheads attended a rally in nearby Shelby County. Four ANF Skinheads were ultimately convicted of the fatal stabbing and were handed heavy sentences, in one case, life in prison.

Since 1989, when the United States Department of Justice (DOJ) established a Skinhead task force within its Civil Rights Division, DOJ has been effective in prosecuting the young hatemongers and in bringing national attention to the problem.* Perhaps the most prominent such case took place in California

---

* Federal law enforcement recently received a powerful weapon for their arsenal: penalty enhancement for hate crimes. The 1994 crime law calls for increased penalties for Federal crimes where the victim was selected "because of the actual or perceived race, color, religion, national origin, ethnicity, gender, disability, or sexual orientation of any person." The Federal Government thus joins the 34 states (plus the District of Columbia) that have passed laws, many based on an ADL model, that provide for stepped-up penalties for bias-motivated crimes. Since Skinheads most frequently choose their victims based on a credo of hatred for certain groups, penalty enhancement laws should result in longer sentences for these thugs and may help to reduce Skinhead terror in the community.

in July 1993, when eight people were arrested by Federal authorities and charged with a variety of conspiracy offenses in connection with a plan to incite a race war by, among other things, bombing an African-American church, sending a letter-bomb to a rabbi, and assassinating several well-known African-American figures.

Race Warriors

Among those involved in the plan were members of the Fourth Reich Skinheads gang. Two Fourth Reich Skins, Christopher David Fisher, 20, the Skinhead gang's leader, and Carl Daniel Boese, 17, pleaded guilty and received prison terms of eight years and 57 months, respectively. Several other racists pleaded guilty to various weapons and conspiracy charges connected to the plot. Among these were a Skinhead, Geremy Rineman, and his girlfriend, Jill Scarborough, a Skinhead supporter. The couple had earlier been united in an Aryan "wedding" at an Oklahoma "Aryan Fest" in 1990.

During that same summer of 1993, Skinheads in Washington State had aspirations similar to those of their California counterparts. Three Skinheads pleaded guilty to Federal charges in connection with two bombings that were part of a plot to ignite a race war in Washington. One of the men threw a bomb into the Tacoma office of the NAACP, causing damage, but no injuries. The other Skins bombed a gay bar in Seattle. Federal investigators discovered that these acts were merely the prelude to a larger plan to bomb synagogues and civil rights organizations and to attack African-American rap artists. The Skins all had ties to the aforementioned neo-Nazi group, Church of the Creator.

More recently, in July 1994, four members of the Massachusetts-based New Dawn Hammerskins were indicted on Federal charges in connection with a conspiracy to intimidate and interfere with the rights of black and Jewish citizens. The leader of the Skinhead group, the only adult among the defendants, pled guilty and received 46 months imprisonment. Investigation into the case revealed that a longtime member of the Ku Klux Klan had attempted to dispose of evidence relevant to the prosecution. The Klansman, Roy Frankhauser of Reading, Pennsylvania, was convicted and sentenced to 25 months in prison.

American Skinheads do not confine themselves to ethnic hatred. They have been held responsible for several murders — and countless assaults — based on their hatred of homosexuals. Fatal Skinhead attacks on gays have occurred in New York City; San Diego; St. Louis; Salem, Oregon; and Reno, Nevada. Most recently, William Douglas Metz, 36, died after he suffered more than 20 stab wounds in a July 1994 attack in Reno. An informant told police that the attack was a "fag-bashing" by a Skinhead gang. A 21-year-old racist Skinhead pleaded guilty, adding that he had also wanted to carve a swastika on the victim's body but did not have enough time. He received two life sentences without the possibility of parole.

Neo-Nazi Skinheads have killed their non-racist counterparts in gang brawls as well as in unprovoked attacks. In August 1990, a fight between racist and non-racist Skinhead factions in the parking lot of a Sacramento club resulted in the stabbing death of a SHARP (Skinheads Against Racial Prejudice) Skin by a racist member of the Sacramento Skins. In August 1992, two neo-Nazi Skinheads stabbed and bludgeoned to death a 17-year-old non-racist Skinhead of mixed Asian and white background, in Olympia, Washington.

When they cannot find living human beings to assault — or when their courage cannot rise to that level — American Skins have attacked the graves of the departed. A Skinhead and two accomplices were charged with the April 21, 1993, desecration of a Jewish cemetery in Everett, Massachusetts. In addition to overturning 100 tombstones and spray-painting swastikas, the vandals scrawled a birthday salute to Adolf Hitler on a nearby wall. The three were ultimately sentenced to two years imprisonment.

Other Jewish institutions have also been attacked. On March 20, 1994, two Skinheads shot several rounds from a high-powered semi-automatic rifle into the stained glass windows of a Eugene, Oregon, synagogue. The shooters were sentenced to terms of 54 and 57 months imprisonment.

The Berserker

American Skinheads have produced over the years a number of publications; some ran for only a few issues, others continue to circulate. Zines that have been published in the last few years include: *Blood and Honor,* out of Long

Beach, California, an American spin-off of the British publication of the same name; *National Socialist Skinhead,* published in St. Paul, Minnesota; *Iron Will* and *Skinhead Power,* both from North Carolina; and *The Berserker* of Levittown, New York, more a newsletter than a full-fledged zine.

The zines focus on Skinhead music, but racist commentary is injected throughout each issue in editorials and interviews. Typical of the views espoused in these interviews are those of members of the band Das Reich: "We must expose the Zionist-controlled media and institutions to the rest of the White 'sheeple' in America ... we would like to salute all the White Stormtroopers that are fighting daily for our struggle."

Another interview in *Blood and Honor* contained a call for readers to lend support to "P.O.W.s." Among these so-called prisoners-of-war were David Lane and Gary Yarbrough, both currently serving long sentences for their role in the neo-Nazi terrorist group, The Order; and Matthew Hayhow, a Skinhead serving 25 years for armed robbery.

Resistance Records, a major producer of Skinhead music in Detroit, puts out a magazine that focuses on Skinhead music in the United States and Canada. It claims a circulation of "12,000 and growing." The magazine's publisher, George Burdi (a.k.a. George Eric Hawthorne), a Canadian, was convicted of aggravated assault for his part in a 1993 brawl in Ottawa with anti-racist demonstrators. Burdi publishes out of Detroit to avoid Canada's laws against racist material. Typical of the magazine's level of rhetoric is its critique of the film, *Schindler's List*:

> Just what we needed in these hard times, yet another movie about the Holy-Hoax.... Steven Spielberg directs this so-called "spell-binding drama" about you-know-what that has been hailed by critics as a "remarkable accomplishment." The only thing "remarkable" about it is that after all these years, Hollywood is still churning out this garbage. This shit doesn't even belong in our toilets.

Some zines such as *Aryan Revolutionary Front*, published in Castro Valley, California, and *White Order*, out of Aurora, Colorado, are aimed at a more general neo-Nazi readership, but nonetheless promote Skinhead bands and events.

Hate Fests

Bands that play hard-driving oi music and spout manifestoes of hate and violence are a prominent part of the American Skinhead scene. Skinhead music festivals have been held in California, Oklahoma, Pennsylvania, Alabama, Michigan and Wisconsin. As elsewhere across the globe, these festivals are hate-fests that often result in violence against the community and among the Skinheads themselves.

Resistance Records hosted one such festival on September 30, 1994, in Racine, Wisconsin. It was billed as a concert honoring the late Ian Stuart, lead vocalist of the British band Skrewdriver, who died in a car accident in 1993.

The concert featured seven bands — Das Reich (from Wisconsin), Aggravated Assault (New Jersey), Berserkr [*sic*] (Oklahoma), Centurion (Wisconsin), Rahowa (Toronto), Bound For Glory (Minnesota) and the English band No Remorse — and attracted an audience of over 300. After the concert, Joe Rowan, lead singer of the Delaware Skinhead band Nordic Thunder, was killed in a skirmish with black youths in a Racine convenience store. Rowan was eulogized on the cover of *Resistance* magazine with lyrics from one of his own songs:

> I know the truth and I know what is right,
> To destroy the zionist way and keep my land White ...
> I've sworn to protect my people,
> For that I'm crucified,
> I live for my Race and for my Race I will die ...

Bound For Glory is perhaps the most influential American Skinhead band. Led by Ed Wolbank, director of the neo-Nazi Northern Hammer Skins in St. Paul, Minnesota, the band has recorded for Resistance Records and the German Rock-O-Rama label, and has toured in Europe with Skrewdriver. A member of the band summarized the underlying message behind their music: "All of our music has a racial theme and that is 100% White."

Detroit Skinheads boast an active music scene. Two local bands — Max Resist and the Hooligans, and Rival — performed frequently at the West Side Clubhouse in Detroit, which served as the hangout for the Detroit Skinhead gang, the West Side Boot Boys. Out-of-state bands also frequently played at the Clubhouse. Among those advertised to appear in a tribute concert to the slain Joe Rowan were Bound For Glory, Centurion, The Voice, Aggravated Assault and Shamrock. A recent flier, however, announced the closing of the West Side Clubhouse, allegedly for reasons of "security"; it claimed that alternative venues would be found for future concerts "in the Detroit area and elsewhere."

In sum, the United States faces a Skinhead problem that is no less serious than that of many other nations — and much more lethal than most.

YUGOSLAVIA

There is a small but energetic Serbian Skinhead scene in The Federal Republic of Yugoslavia (a country now comprising Serbia and Montenegro). The Skins' focus is on Serbian nationalism, but they also embrace the racism and anti-Semitism of their comrades around the world.

A Yugoslavia-based branch of a United States gang called United White Skinheads is run by Branko Kunovski of Belgrade. Kunovski, in a letter he wrote, took credit for vandalizing a Belgrade synagogue with Nazi stickers from

Gary Lauck's Nebraska-based NSDAP-AO and boasted that he booby-trapped them with hidden razors. Kunovski also runs *Predskazanje* (Prediction), a skinzine, and distributes Serbian Skinhead music internationally. The British skinzine *Last Chance* reports a "massive" "oi" music scene in Serbia that includes several nationalist Skinhead bands. Ritam Nereda (Rhythm of Disorder) is the most well-known: they sing some songs in English and have received favorable reviews in American and British skinzines. In a 1993 issue of *Dixie Rose*, a now-defunct skinzine from Texas, Boban, the band's singer, described his outlook on recent Yugoslav history:

> We think about ourselves as victims of the so called "New World Movement." If the United (Z.O.G.)* Nations hadn't fucked us up everything would be over. We would have our territory back, have saved our people, stopped the Muslims from conquering Europe again, and the war would've ended a long time ago.

Other popular bands are Directori (Directors) and Generacija Bez Buducnosti (Generation Without a Future). The Detroit-based zine *Resistance* reports that videos of these bands as well as Ritam Nereda have been shown on television.

---

* Z.O.G., or Zionist Occupied Government, is a term used mainly by American extremists to indicate Jewish domination of the government.

GLOSSARY

Cabezas Rapadas

Literally, "shaved heads." The term used for Skinheads in some, but not all, Spanish-speaking countries.

Casuals

Like the **Hooligans,** casuals are violent youths who occasionally carry out Skinhead-like attacks, often at soccer stadiums and surrounding areas. While they affect an appearance similar to Skinheads and some-times exhibit racist and anti-Semitic attitudes, they are not usually dedicated to Nazism. Casuals are primarily a French phenomenon.

Church of the Creator (COTC)

A virulently racist and anti-Semitic organization that uses the rhetoric of religion as a camouflage for the promotion of hate. It was very influential among American Skinheads until recently, when it became inactive in the United States. It retains some influence among Skinheads abroad, notably in Sweden.

Doc Martens

The brand name of British-made combat-style boots that are essential to the Skinhead uniform. They are a favorite weapon of the Skinheads who employ them in group assaults that they call "boot parties."

88

A common neo-Nazi slogan signifying "Heil Hitler," H being the eighth letter of the alphabet.

Hooligans

Sometimes "hools." Predominantly a European phenomenon, hooligans are violent soccer fans who often dress like Skinheads and spout racist chants in stadiums. Occasionally, Skinheads and hooligans jointly engage in violent rampages. For practical purposes, it is often difficult to distinguish between the groups.

Lauck, Gary

The Nebraska-based world-wide distributor of Nazi propaganda in 12 languages. Through the NSDAP-AO or National Socialist German Workers Party-Overseas Organization (the initials come from the name in German), Lauck's materials are commonly found among Skinheads around the world.

NSDAP-AO

See Lauck, Gary.

Odinism

A pre-Christian European religion that involves worship of the Norse god Odin. Many neo-Nazis, including Skinheads, regard themselves as adherents to Odinism.

Oi

An English Cockney expression, equivalent to "hey!" It is the name for the type of hard-driving rock music favored by Skinheads, both neo-Nazi and non-racist.

The Order

An American racist and anti-Semitic terrorist organization, many of whose members are currently serving lengthy prison sentences.

Roma

A term for the ethnic group commonly known as Gypsies.

SHARP

An acronym for "Skinheads Against Racial Prejudice," an anti-racist Skinhead group that exists in several countries. SHARP Skinheads resemble racist Skinheads in appearance and demeanor but belong to sometimes multi-racial gangs that, on occasion, engage in fights with racist Skinheads.

Skinzine

A contraction of "Skinhead" and "magazine." Usually a crudely written home-published newsletter that focuses on Skinhead bands and their recordings as well as other elements of the Skinhead scene. Sometimes called "zine" for short. Skinzines vary widely in quality and frequency of publication.

White Aryan Resistance (WAR)

A hate group founded by Tom Metzger of Fallbrook, California, and run by him and his son, John Metzger. It is influential among Skinheads in the USA and abroad.

A NOTE ON SOURCES

This 18-month global study was conducted in three stages: the first, a worldwide search for experts willing to participate in our project; the second, collection and analysis of the data; the third, a return to our sources to update our information and confirm its accuracy.

Our contacts included Jewish communal institutions, human rights organizations, law enforcement agencies, university-based research centers, defectors and confidential sources. An abundance of information also came from the ADL collection of Skinhead publications and recordings.

Estimating Skinhead numbers has not been a simple task. The Skinhead phenomenon is more a way of life than a structured movement: there are no "official" Skinhead organizations, and there is no such thing as "membership" in the ordinary sense of the term. The entire Skinhead scene is a congeries of informal relationships — among activists and their supporters, and among the gangs, both nationally and internationally. Nevertheless, it has been possible to make reasonable estimates by tallying Skinhead numbers at rallies, marches, concerts, festivals, soccer matches and other gatherings.

A word of caution: This is not a comprehensive study of right-wing extremist activity around the world. Obviously, there are far-right forces other than Skinheads at work in many countries. Where ties exist between Skins and these extremists, they have been addressed in the report. Yet the Skinheads' shared characteristics and international connections make them a fit subject for consideration on their own.

Sources

The Anti-Defamation League gratefully acknowledges the contributions to this report of the following organizations and individuals:

Australia/Israel Publications
B'nai B'rith Anti-Defamation Commission, Australia
B'nai B'rith, District 26, Argentina
B'nai B'rith Luxembourg
The Board of Deputies of British Jews — Community Security
    Organisation
Bundesamt für Verfassungsschutz (Federal Office for the Protection of
    the Constitution), Germany
Centre de Recherche et de Documentation sur l'Antisemitisme, Paris
Documentation Center of B'nai B'rith, Spain
Documentation Center "Raúl Bitrán" of District 27 of B'nai B'rith, Chile
Dokumentationsarchiv des österreichischen Widerstandes
    (Austrian Resistance Archives)
European Centre for Research and Action on Racism and
    Antisemitism (CERA), Paris
Executive Council of Australian Jewry

Freedom House, New York
Human Rights Watch, New York
Institute of Jewish Affairs, London
Jewish Community of Helsinki
The Jewish Historical Institute in Poland
League for Human Rights of B'nai Brith Canada
National Endowment for Democracy, Washington, D.C.
Oficina Relaciones Humanas, B'nai B'rith, Bogota, Colombia
Public Policy Institute, Hungary
Radio Free Europe/Radio Liberty Research Institute
Ritzaus Bureau, the National Danish Newsagency
South African Jewish Board of Deputies
Tel Aviv University — Project for the Study of Anti-Semitism

Vivienne Anstey, South Africa
Richard J. Berman, Canada
Philippe Broussard, France
Jan Brygfjell, Norway
Alina Cala, Poland
Perla Copernik, Brazil
Rainer Erb, Germany
Cathy Feldman, Japan
Konstanty Gebert, Poland
Hugo Gijsels, Belgium
Annette Gladwin, Australia
Dayan Gross, South Africa
Judith Ingram, Hungary
Jeremy Jones, Australia
Dan Kantor, Finland

Paul Katow, Luxembourg
Daniel McAdams, Hungary
John Micgiel, Poland
Matthias Mletzko, Germany
Patrick Moreau, Germany
Laurent Murawiec, France
Lisa Palmieri-Billig, Italy
Arch Puddington, New York
Sándor Révész, Hungary
Philip Sampson, Denmark
Ivan Sellei, Hungary
Thomas Szayna, Czech Republic
Dr. Szabolcs Szita, Hungary
Gideon Taylor, New York
Bernd Wagner, Germany

In addition, this report benefitted from the invaluable assistance of the following ADL staff members: Robert Goldmann, ADL European Representative; Elliot Welles, Associate Director, European Affairs; Dorothy A. Rose, Research Analyst, Research & Evaluation Department; and Yvonne Mentore, secretary, Fact Finding Department.

Anti-Defamation League of B'nai B'rith

NATIONAL OFFICE
823 United Nations Plaza, New York, NY 10017 ....(212) 490-2525
WASHINGTON OFFICE
1100 Connecticut Avenue, N.W. (Suite 1020), Washington, D.C. 20036.......................(202) 452-8320

REGIONAL OFFICES
ALBUQUERQUE
P.O. Box 21639, Albuquerque, NM 87154..(505) 823-2712
ARIZONA
The First Interstate Tower, 3550 North Central Avenue (Suite 914),
Phoenix, AZ 85012 ....(602) 274-0991
ATLANTA (Southeast)
One Securities Centre, 3490 Piedmont Road N.E. (Suite 610), Atlanta, GA 30305 ....(404) 262-3470
BOSTON (New England)
126 High Street, 4th Floor, Boston, MA 02110...(617) 457-8800
CHICAGO (Greater Chicago/Wisconsin)
309 West Washington, (Suite 750), Chicago, IL 60606 ....(312) 782-5080
CLEVELAND (Northern Ohio)
505 Terminal Tower, Cleveland, OH 44113 ....(216) 579-9600
COLUMBUS (Ohio/Indiana/Kentucky)
42 East Gay St., (Suite 814), Columbus, OH 43215 ....(614) 621-0601
CONNECTICUT
419 Whalley Avenue, New Haven, CT 06511 ....(203) 787-4281
DALLAS (Northwest Texas/Oklahoma)
12800 Hillcrest Road (Suite 219), Dallas, TX 75230 ....(214) 960-0342
D.C. (D.C./MARYLAND)
1100 Connecticut Avenue, N.W. (Suite 1020), Washington, D.C. 20036......................(202) 452-8310
DENVER (Mountain States)
300 South Dahlia Street (Suite 202), Denver, CO 80222...(303) 321-7177
DETROIT (Michigan)
4000 Town Center (Suite 420), Southfield, MI 48075-1405 ....(810) 355-3730
HOUSTON (Southwest)
4635 Southwest Freeway (Suite 400), Houston, TX 77027..(713) 627-3490
LOS ANGELES (Pacific Southwest)
10495 Santa Monica Boulevard, Los Angeles, CA 90025...(310) 446-8000
MIAMI (Florida)
150 SE Second Avenue (Suite 800), Miami, FL 33131 ....(305) 373-6306
NEW JERSEY
743 Northfield Avenue, West Orange, NJ 07052 ....(201) 669-9700
NEW ORLEANS (South Central)
925 Common Street (Suite 975), New Orleans, LA 70112 ....(504) 522-9534
NEW YORK CITY (New York City, Westchester, Rockland, Putnam and Long Island)
823 United Nations Plaza, New York, NY 10017 ....(212) 885-7970
NEW YORK STATE
125 Wolf Rd. (Suite 504), Albany, NY 12205 ....(518) 446-0038
OMAHA (Plains States)
333 South 132 Street, Omaha, NE 68154 ....(402) 333-1303
ORANGE COUNTY
2700 North Main Street (Suite 500), Santa Ana, CA 92701..(714) 973-4733
PALM BEACH COUNTY
The Commerce Center, 324 Datura Street (Suite 223),
West Palm Beach, FL 33401 ....(407) 832-7144
PHILADELPHIA (Eastern Pennsylvania/Delaware)
230 South Broad Street, 20th Floor, Philadelphia, PA 19102 ....(215) 735-4267
SAN DIEGO
7851 Mission Center Court (Suite 320), San Diego, CA 92108 ....(619) 293-3770
SAN FRANCISCO (Central Pacific)
720 Market Street (Suite 800), San Francisco, CA 94102-2501 ....(415) 981-3500
SEATTLE (Pacific Northwest)
Plaza 600 Building (Suite 720), 600 Stewart Street, Seattle, WA 98101 ....(206) 448-5349
ST. LOUIS (Missouri/Southern Illinois)
10926 Schuetz Road, St. Louis, MO 63146 ....(314) 432-6868
VIRGINIA/NORTH CAROLINA
6330 Newtown Rd. (Suite 326), Norfolk, VA 23502 ....(804) 455-9002

OVERSEAS OFFICES
JERUSALEM
30 King David Street, Jerusalem, Israel 94101 011-972-2-251-171
CANADA
Cooperative Association with the League for Human Rights of Canadian B'nai Brith
15 Hove Street (Suite 210), Downsview, Ontario, Canada, M3H 4Y8 ....(416) 633-6227